Entrepreneur

MAGAZINE'S

POCKET GUIDES

Mutual Funds
A QUICK
START GUIDE

Entrepreneur Press and
Jason R. Rich

EP
Entrepreneur Press

Editorial Director: Jere L. Calmes
Cover Design: Beth Hansen-Winter
Editorial and Production Services: CWL Publishing Enterprises, Inc.,
Madison, WI, www.cwlpub.com

ISBN   13: 978-1-59918-062-5
       10: 1 -59918-062-6

Registred with the Library of Congress

12 11 10 09 08 07   10 9 8 7 6 5 4 3 2

Contents

Introduction   vii

Chapter 1

Mutual Fund Basics   1

What Is a Mutual Fund?   3
How Mutual Funds Work   12
Ten Important Mutual Fund Facts   17
Reasons to Start Investing Right Now   24

Chapter 2

Defining Your Investment Goals   27

Analyze Your Current Financial Situation   29
Financial Worksheets   30
Calculate How Much Money You Can Use
    to Start Investing   36
Define Your Short-Term and Long-Term Goals   37
Decide How Much Risk You're Willing to Accept   46
Gather Your Funds to Get Started Investing   50

Chapter 3

Getting the Investment Help You Need — 51

Who Needs an Investment Advisor? — 54
Selecting Your Investment Advisor — 56
The ABCs of CFAs, CFPs, CPAs, ChFCs, and RIAs — 57
Questions to Ask a Potential Investment Advisor — 60
Understanding the Fees You'll Pay — 65
Advice from an Expert: Stuart Ritter, CFP — 67

Chapter 4

The Anatomy of a Mutual Fund — 82

Types of Mutual Funds by Strategy — 84
Categories of Mutual Funds by Their Primary Holdings — 85
Fund Type: Risks and Returns — 96
Why Portfolio Asset Allocation Is Important — 98
The Shareholder Report/Annual Report — 108
Six Things to Know About a Fund Before Investing — 111
Exchange-Traded Funds: An Alternative to Mutual Funds — 114
Advice from an Expert: Larry J. Puglia, Fund Manager — 116

Chapter 5

Researching Mutual Funds — 124

Why Research Is Important — 127
What You Can Learn from Researching Funds — 129
Narrow Your Search Using a Fund Selection Tool — 131
Other Useful Research and Analytical Tools — 134
Tools and Publications Offered by Morningstar, Inc. — 137
Sources of Current Quotes and Financial Data — 140
Advice from an Expert: Christine Benz,
 Mutual Fund Analyst — 143

Chapter 6

Get Started Investing Now   **154**

Choosing Your Mutual Fund Company   156
Mutual Fund Company Contact Information   159
Solidifying Your Investment Goals and Plans   159
How to Establish Your Account   162
Taking Care of Your Portfolio   170

Chapter 7

Managing Your Portfolio   **173**

The Ten Basic Steps to Mutual Fund Investing   175
How to Manage Your Portfolio Properly   176
Gather and Enter All Pertinent Information   177
The Portfolio Management Tool Offered by
    Your Mutual Fund Company   180
The Portfolio Management Tool Offered by Morningstar   180
Additional Portfolio Management Tools You Can Use   184
Advice from an Expert: John Flora, Senior Product
    Manager for Quicken   186
What Managing a Mutual Fund Portfolio Entails   190
Advice from an Expert: Michael McLaughlin, CFP and ChFC   193
Final Thoughts   199

Appendix A

Recommended Reading   **203**

Appendix B

Glossary   **211**

Index   **231**

Introduction

If you're interested in investing in mutual funds, this *Entrepreneur Magazine's Pocket Guide* provides the information you need to get started quickly! This book covers only mutual funds—not other types of investments that might fit into your portfolio.

Right from the start, it's important to understand that mutual funds do *not* offer a get-rich-quick opportunity. They are an ideal long-term investment tool, especially if you're saving for a major life event, such as buying a home, paying for your child's college education, or saving for retirement.

Because mutual funds are investments, they carry some level of risk. In other words, they're not insured by the Federal Deposit Insurance Corporation (FDIC) or guaranteed to make you money. While it's extremely unlikely you'd ever lose all of your invested money, you could potentially lose some of your principal. Since mutual funds are diversified, they're a lot less risky than investing in individual stocks or many other types of investments. And, if you pick the right combination of funds, you could generate impressive returns and build significant wealth over time.

From this book, you'll learn the basics about what mutual funds are and how they work (Chapter 1), how to define your investment goals (Chapter 2), the importance of choosing a reliable and experienced investment advisor (Chapter 3), how various types of mutual funds perform differently, based on market conditions and other factors (Chapter 4), how to research specific mutual funds before investing in them (Chapter 5), how to get started investing quickly and easily (Chapter 6), and how to manage your investment portfolio over the long term (Chapter 7).

To make this book easier to understand, particularly for novice investors, throughout each chapter you'll see "Investing Tips." These are tidbits of information intended to help you become a better investor and make smarter investment-related decisions. You'll also see "Mutual Fund Key

Term" boxes, which define the key mutual fund-related terms you'll need to understand in order to become a savvy investor.

The "Warning" boxes scattered throughout this book will help you avoid common pitfalls and mistakes. Throughout this book you'll also find information about dozens of Web sites and other valuable resources of interest to novice mutual fund investors.

Another benefit of this book is that you'll be able to learn from the experiences of some highly reputable mutual fund experts, from companies like T. Rowe Price, The Vanguard Group, and Morningstar. From in-depth and exclusive interviews, you'll obtain additional investing insight, plus strategies and advice to help you generate better returns from your mutual fund investments.

Like all of the books in *Entrepreneur Magazine's Pocket Guide* series, this one is designed to be easy to understand and take you less than three to four hours to read. So, if you find this book to be informative and helpful, be sure to check out some of the other books in this popular series, which include: *Dirty Little Secrets: What the Credit Bureaus Won't Tell You; Why Rent? Own Your Dream Home;* and *Mortgages and Refinancing: Get The Best Rates.* These books are available from bookstores everywhere or through the Entrepreneur Press Web site (*www.entrepeneurpress.com*).

As you begin to learn about mutual fund investing, remember that it's extremely important to define your investment goals and time horizon (concepts you'll learn about shortly) and to make sure those goals and your expectations are realistic. If you're expecting to generate a 20- to 30-percent annual return on your mutual fund investments, for example, that's not realistic for most investors. Also, it's essential that you thoroughly understand exactly what you're investing in.

Investing Tip

SUGGESTIONS WORTH FOLLOWING In Chapter 7, you'll read a section called "The 10 Basic Steps to Mutual Fund Investing." To help ensure your success, be sure to follow these steps, without skipping any of them.

Finally, if you'd like to share your thoughts or investing success story with this book's author, you can visit his Web site at www.JasonRich.com or e-mail him at jr7777@aol.com.

By picking up this book, you've taken the first step necessary to start making your money work harder for you and to enable it to potentially grow at a faster rate than if you were to put it into a bank savings account, a money market account, or a Certificate of Deposit, for example. Now, if you're ready to start learning all about mutual fund investing, simply turn the page!

CHAPTER 1

Mutual Fund Basics

WHAT'S IN THIS CHAPTER

- What a mutual fund is—and is not
- How mutual funds work
- Mutual fund facts
- Why people invest in mutual funds

So, you're interested in investing in mutual funds? Well, you're not alone! According to research conducted by Investment Company Institute (www.ici.org), as of July 2006, $9.377 trillion was invested in over 8,454 mutual funds by investors within the United States. This represented a $900 billion increase over 2004. Worldwide investment in mutual funds (as of 2005) was $17.8 trillion.

For a multitude of reasons, mutual funds provide an excellent investment opportunity for people from all walks of life. In recent years, the popularity of mutual funds as an investment opportunity has grown dramatically. In the United States, as of 2005, 92 million individuals (approximately one in three adult Americans), representing more than 54 million households, were mutual fund investors.

This book is all about mutual funds—what they are, why they provide such a solid investment opportunity for so many people, and how to get started as an investor. The goal of this book is to provide you with a comprehensive introduction to mutual funds, so if you decide to invest in them, you'll be able to make intelligent decisions based on your financial goals.

If you've never invested before, this book will help you get started, whether or not you choose to solicit the help and advice of an *investment advisor* (a topic covered in Chapter 3). If you're already an investor, this book will help you understand how to better manage your portfolio and hopefully earn better returns from your mutual fund investments.

Warning

THERE'S ALWAYS RISK The first and perhaps most important lesson to learn is that investing in mutual funds involves some level of *risk*. This is *not* a guaranteed money-making opportunity. Unlike a savings account at a bank, for example, most mutual fund investments are *not* protected or insured by the Federal Deposit Insurance Corporation (FDIC). While the risk associated with investing in mutual funds is lower than with other types of investments (for reasons that will be explored later in this book), the value of your mutual fund investments could potentially decrease, resulting in financial loss.

RISK In terms of investing, risk is the measurable possibility that you will lose money or that your investment will not increase in value. It involves both uncertainty and exposure. Some types of investments are inherently  Mutual Fund Key Term
riskier than others. One way to reduce risk is through diversification. Mutual funds reduce investment risk, because their portfolios are typically composed of a diverse selection of holdings. Some mutual funds, however, are significantly riskier than others. As a general rule (although it doesn't apply 100 percent of the time), the riskier an investment, the greater the potential return on investment. To maintain your emotional sanity, it's vital that you be comfortable with the level of risk you assume when investing. This is your *risk tolerance*.

What Is a Mutual Fund?

A *mutual fund* is an investment vehicle consisting of stocks, bonds, short-term money market instruments, securities, and other assets maintained by a company that invests funds from a pool of money from many individual and institutional investors. The investments owned by the fund are its *holdings*. The collection of holdings, controlled by the fund's manager, is a *portfolio*. Mutual funds offer an easy way for an investor to invest in many securities at once (to obtain *diversification*). Fund shares are purchased by investors directly from the fund or a broker who represents the fund.

Mutual Fund Key Term

PORTFOLIO Either a collection of holdings of a mutual fund or a collection of investments held by an individual—stocks, bonds, mutual funds, and other securities and assets (including cash).

DIVERSIFICATION The distribution of an investment portfolio across different investments as a strategy to reduce risk. This strategy applies the wisdom of that old saying, "Don't put all your eggs into one basket." When a portfolio is diversified, if one investment declines in value, the chances are that the values of other investments will rise and offset that loss, since types of investments perform differently in various market or economic conditions. A well-diversified mutual fund portfolio would typically consist of stock funds, bond funds, and money market funds. It could be further diversified by investing in domestic, international, global, and/or sector- or industry-specific funds.

When you invest in a fund, you acquire shares in that fund. The number of shares you own represents your proportionate ownership in the fund's holdings. As you'll discover in Chapter 4, there are several types of mutual funds. Each fund type (which is based on its types of holdings) has a different level of risk, a different focus, and different management philosophies. (Chapter 4 describes the various types of mutual funds in detail.)

When you buy into a mutual fund, the price you pay per share for that fund is based on its *net asset value* (*NAV*), plus any fees (such as sales commissions) that are incurred. All of the different fees and costs associated with mutual fund investing will be explored later. Ultimately, once you know what fees you're responsible for (information you can obtain from a fund's *prospectus*), you can calculate how those costs will impact your investment using a Mutual Fund Cost Calculator, like the one found at The Securities & Exchange Commission's Web site (*www.sec.gov/investor/tools.shtml*).

NET ASSET VALUE (NAV) The share price of a mutual fund. The NAV is calculated daily by adding up the values of all of the holdings in the fund portfolio and then subtracting any expenses associated with the management of the fund. This total value is then divided by the number of shares. Unlike a stock, a mutual fund can have an unlimited and ever-changing number of shares.

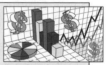

Mutual Fund Key Term

An investment's *total return percentage* is a measure of how much it has grown or declined in value during a specific time period. For example, when you look at a fund's performance, you may find its *total return percentage* for the year to date (YTD) and for the past 12 months, three years, five years, ten

Investment Tips

OWNING FRACTIONS It is possible for investors to own a fraction of a mutual fund share. In fact, it's very common. For example, if you invest $5,000 in a fund that has a NAV of $34.65, you're purchasing 144.30 shares of that fund, assuming there are no initial fees, such as a sales commission.

OPEN-END FUNDS Most mutual funds are *open-end* funds. This means that an unlimited number of investors can acquire an unlimited number of shares in that fund. A *closed-end* fund means that the fund's manager has determined the number of shares that will be issued. Once those shares have been sold, the only way to buy shares is to buy them directly from a shareholder—not from the fund, as with an open-end fund. However, it is also possible for an open-end fund to stop accepting new investors.

years, and/or since the fund was established (its inception date). Obviously, a positive number for the total return percentage is always good. All investors seek a high positive return on investment. When a fund posts its total return percentages, they are calculated as if all *dividends* and *capital gains* are reinvested in the fund.

A mutual fund's *rate of return* is a measure of what an investor would have earned had he or she owned shares in the fund for that period. The rate of return helps an investor learn about a fund's past performance (also called *historical performance*), which is not necessarily, however, an indicator of how the fund will perform in the future.

Looking at a fund's past performance can provide insight into a fund's stability and long-term potential for success.

DIVIDEND Payment by a stock-issuing company of a portion of earnings to its shareholders, determined by the board of directors. (Companies are not obligated to pay dividends.) Dividends can be paid in cash or in more  **Mutual Fund Key Term** stock. A dividend may be quoted in terms of the dollar amount for each share (*dividends per share*, DPS) or in terms of a percent of the current market price (*dividend yield*). When a mutual fund's holdings include stocks and those stocks pay dividends, the fund must pass those dividends along to the fund's investors annually. An investor must pay tax on this income. However, an investor has the option to automatically reinvest dividend payments to acquire more shares.

CAPITAL GAIN (LOSS) An increase (decrease) in the value of a *capital asset* that puts that value above (below) the purchase cost. This gain (loss) is not realized (treated as real) until the capital asset is sold. A capital gain may **Mutual Fund Key Term** be short term (one year or less) or long term (more than one year) and must be claimed as income. A mutual fund buys and sells investment assets. When a sale generates a profit and the asset was held by the fund for more than one year, that profit is capital gain, which is passed on to you as a capital gain distribution. You receive a Form 1099-DIV for the distribution, which is taxed as a long-term capital gain regardless of how long you have owned the shares in the mutual fund.

Another tool investors use to evaluate and analyze funds is independent ratings from highly respected mutual fund analyst companies, like Morningstar. Chapter 5 offers more information on how to research specific mutual funds using a

Mutual Fund Key Term

CAPITAL GAINS DISTRIBUTION The money paid by a mutual fund to each of its investors based on profits generated by the funds investments. Capital gains distributions are typically distributed annually and reported on a Form 1099-DIV. The distribution is taxed as a long-term capital gain regardless of how long the investor has owned the shares in the mutual fund. Instead of receiving payment, an investor can opt to reinvest the capital gain distribution to acquire additional shares of the fund.

variety of tools and resources, including those offered by Morningstar.

Every mutual fund has one of the following overall objectives:

- **Growth.** This type of fund is intended to increase significantly in value and generate high returns. This is typically ideal for a long-term investment strategy, when you have ten, 20, or more years before you'll need to access the money you've invested. These funds tend to pay little or no dividends.

- **Income.** These are funds that are intended to generate a stream of income in the form of dividends and capital gains distributions. The investor has the option to receive a check regularly.

- **Growth and Income.** These funds have a dual goal, to generate long-term growth and an income for investors.

- **Preservation of Capital.** These funds tend to be much less risky. They're ideal for shorter-term investments when the investor can't afford to lose any of his or her principal, but doesn't expect extremely high returns on the investment.

Advantages of Mutual Fund Investing

Unlike an investment in an individual stock, bond, or other type of *security*, a mutual fund offers a wide range of advantages that help to protect the investor's money. These advantages include the following:

- **Security.** An investment product or vehicle that represents ownership, such as a mutual fund, stock, bond, option, or other type of financial asset.
- **Affordability and Accessibility.** Investing in mutual funds requires relatively little money, so almost anyone can start quickly and with relative ease.
- **Diversification.** One of the most important investment strategies taught to all investors is *diversification*. As mentioned earlier, by spreading investments across a range of companies, industries, or sectors, investors can dramatically lower their risk. If you own 30 stocks, for example, and some decrease in value, others will potentially increase to balance out the loss. In contrast, if you invested in only one or two stocks and those stocks dramatically dropped in value, it would represent a significant loss. Mutual funds offer diversification by maintaining a portfolio often composed of dozens of stocks, bonds, assets, or other types of securities.

- **Liquidity.** Mutual funds are considered *liquid* investments, meaning an investor can quickly and easily sell his or her shares and receive cash. (The fund *redeems*—buys back—your shares.) The price received for the redemption of shares will be the fund's current (end of day) NAV, minus any fees associated with the redemption. An investor can redeem shares of mutual funds at any time, for any reason. (If the mutual fund investment is part of a retirement plan, special redemption rules apply, which will be explored later.)

- **Professional Management.** Every mutual fund has a professional *fund manager* who is responsible for managing the money invested in that fund, conducting research, selecting investments for the fund's portfolio, and then monitoring the performance of the fund on a daily basis. (Later in this book, you'll read an in-depth interview with a fund manager and learn more about what they do and how they do it.)

- **Regulation.** There are laws and guidelines fund managers must follow. This regulation is overseen by the Securities and Exchange Commission.

Potential Drawbacks of Mutual Funds

While there are many benefits to investing in mutual funds, there are a few drawbacks. The biggest drawback is potentially the fees involved. Regardless of whether the fund's NAV increases or decreases, an investor is responsible for paying

FUND MANAGER The person responsible for managing the money invested in a specific mutual fund and overseeing the day-to-day operation of that fund. The fund manager, with the help of analysts, decides how a fund's assets will be invested and what investment strategies will be used. When evaluating a mutual fund as a potential investment, consider the fund manager's experience, education, track record, investment strategy, and tenure managing that fund.

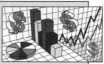

Mutual Fund Key Term

LIQUIDITY The ease with which an investment can be converted into cash. Cash—whether held in a traditional savings or checking account or stored under a mattress—is the most liquid asset, because that money is readily available whenever you need it. A mutual fund investment is considered extremely liquid, because you can redeem your shares and receive cash quickly.

various fees associated with acquiring and redeeming fund shares and managing the fund. If you're not careful, the fees associated with a fund can add up and dramatically impact your ability to profit from your mutual fund investments.

It's also important to understand that any money you earn from your mutual fund investments is taxable. You'll need to pay taxes on *dividends* and *capital gains distribution* while you own the shares and on any profits you earn when you redeem shares in a fund.

Another potential drawback to investing in a mutual fund is that an individual investor has no control whatsoever over which investments make up the fund's portfolio. It's the fund manager who controls the fund's portfolio and makes all decisions related to the fund's management and holdings.

Investing Tip

MORE TO COME Strategies for calculating, managing, and potentially reducing fees associated with mutual fund investing will be explored later.

When an investor purchases or redeems shares of a fund, he or she doesn't know exactly what the purchase or redemption price per share will be until the end of that business day. Unlike stocks, for example, whose prices fluctuate throughout the day when the stock exchange is open, a mutual fund's NAV is calculated once per day, at the end of the day, after the major exchanges close.

The NAV is only one way to measure the strength of a fund and whether it represents a good investment or not. The fund's *total return* during a specific period takes into account changes in a fund's NAV as a result of appreciation or depreciation (rise or drop in value) of its holdings, payment of any income or capital gains distributions, and reinvestment of all distributions. How to analyze the performance of a fund is described within Chapter 5.

How Mutual Funds Work

A mutual fund is easier to invest in than other types of investments, such as individual stocks, bonds, or other securities. This is because someone else (the fund's manager) is responsible for doing all of the research and fund management work for you. While it's a good idea to check your mutual fund portfolio periodically and manage your investments (a topic covered in Chapter 7), there's no need to watch those investments throughout each and every day.

Here's the best way to invest in a mutual fund. First, sit down and figure out your investment goals. Decide what you want to get out of the investment over the short term and the long term. The time you'll have your money invested is your *time horizon.* Next, you'll want to determine how much risk you're willing to take when investing your money. This will help you decide on the type(s) of mutual funds. Chapter 2 focuses on defining your investing goals.

TIME HORIZON The length of time you'll be investing in order to reach a specific investment goal.

Mutual Fund Key Term

After you determine how much money you have to invest to get started and decide if you'll continue to invest an additional amount each month (an *automatic investment plan*), you can begin choosing specific mutual funds. The best way to do this is with the help of an *investment advisor* (see Chapter 3) and/or by conducting your own research about specific mutual funds.

When working with an investment advisor, it's important to understand whom he or she represents and how he or she is being compensated for advice and/or services. Investment advisors may recommend stocks, bonds, mutual funds, or other SEC-registered investments for clients. An investment

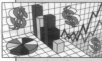

INVESTMENT ADVISOR Someone who helps an investor make investment decisions. This person can represent individual investors and charge a fee or can represent specific

Mutual Fund Key Term investment products, such as mutual funds, and generate sales commissions from selling investment products. Most mutual fund companies also employ salaried investment advisors who offer advice to clients.

advisor can possess any of a wide range of accreditations or certifications. An advisor might be a Certified Financial Planner or Certified Public Accountant, for example, but this is not necessarily a requirement.

As you'll discover from Chapter 5, there are many resources available to help you research specific mutual funds. The decisions you make about which funds to invest in should be based in large part on the extent to which they seem likely to help you achieve your financial goals within your time horizon.

As you know, when you buy shares in a mutual fund, that money you invest will be pooled with money from thousands of other investors. The fund's manager will invest that money in a diversified group of stocks, bonds, and other securities and follow a specific investment strategy or philosophy that is outlined in the fund's *prospectus*. (You can obtain a fund's prospectus from the mutual fund company directly or from a fund's broker. The easiest and fastest way to obtain a prospectus is online, from the mutual fund company's Web site. You can also call the fund's toll-free number or submit a request by mail or, if the fund has an office or a customer service center nearby, you can pick up a prospectus in person.) Every mutual fund has a board of directors who oversee the work of the fund's manager to ensure that he or she is keeping with the overall objectives and investment philosophies of that fund.

PROSPECTUS A document that contains information about a specific mutual fund, including its costs, investment objectives, risks, details about the fund's manager, and information about the fund's past performance. You should read the prospectus thoroughly before investing.

Mutual Fund Key Term

Over the time you own shares in a mutual fund, you can earn money in three ways.

First, your fund can make dividend payments. That means you earn money when the fund earns income in the form of dividends and interest from the securities held in its portfolio.

Second, you could benefit from capital gains distributions, if the fund sells assets that have increased in value and generated a profit. At the end of the year, most funds distribute these earnings to investors in the form of capital gains. (For the investor, this could be taxable income, depending on the situation.) Many investors opt to automatically reinvest dividends and capital gains distributions, to buy additional shares in the fund. The alternative is for the fund to send you a check for your dividend and/or capital gains distributions.

Third, you can benefit from investing in mutual funds when the fund's NAV rises above the price you paid to purchase your shares. If you redeem your shares at a price higher than what you paid per share, you've earned a positive return on your investment (assuming you've taken fees and taxes into account).

When you hold shares of a mutual fund, you benefit from the fund's manager overseeing that fund's investments for you. You are responsible, however, for paying your share of the fund's overall operating expenses. All of these operational fees, including the fund manager's salary, will be described within the fund's *prospectus*.

Investing Tip

RULES OF THE GAME When a mutual fund carries a name that suggests a specific type of investment strategy or focus, the SEC requires that at least 80 percent of that fund's holdings be directly related to that implied strategy or focus. The other 20 percent of its holdings, however, can be invested into other types of securities, at the fund manager's discretion. For example, according to the prospectus for Fidelity Investments' Spartan 500 Index Fund, this specific fund "seeks investment results that correspond to the total return (i.e. the combination of capital changes and income) of common stocks publicly traded in the United States, as represented by the Standard & Poor's 500 Index (S&P 500), while keeping transaction costs and other expenses low. ... Principal investment strategies include normally investing at least 80 percent of assets in common stocks included in the S&P 500."

Mutual Fund Key Term

EXPENSE RATIO A measure of a mutual fund's total annual expenses expressed as a percentage of the fund's net assets. The lower the expense ratio, the better for the investor.

At any time, you can redeem your shares and receive cash for the sale (within seven business days, usually faster). Your ability to redeem shares is restricted somewhat if you invested as part of an IRA or other type of retirement account or plan.

To help build your investment portfolio, most mutual fund companies offer an *automatic investment plan,* which allows for a predetermined amount of money to be deducted from your checking account each month to be invested directly into the mutual fund(s) you've specified. The benefits to this type of investment strategy, which incorporates *dollar cost averaging,* will be explored later. You'll be reading many tips and strategies for picking mutual funds and then managing your investment portfolio throughout this book, especially in Chapters 5 and 7.

DOLLAR COST AVERAGING An investment strategy that consists of investing an equal amount of money every month in a fund, regardless of whether the price is high or low. When the price is low, you'll be buying more shares than when the price is high. This strategy reduces the average price you pay per share over time, but it does not guarantee a profit or prevent losses. When you sign up for an automatic investment plan, you'll be taking advantage of dollar cost averaging.

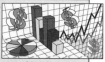

Mutual Fund Key Term

Ten Important Mutual Fund Facts

The following are ten important facts you should understand about mutual funds *before* investing in them:

Investing Tip

GOVERNMENT'S SHARE You must pay income taxes on dividends and interest payments you receive from a mutual fund. When you redeem shares, you're responsible for a capital gains tax on any profit you've earned from the sale. You may also be responsible for paying taxes on the fund's capital gains. Different tax rules apply to different types of funds.

1. There is some risk associated with investing in mutual funds. The level of risk, however, varies depending on factors such as the type of mutual fund. Mutual funds sold by banks (including money market funds) are not considered deposits and are *not* insured by the FDIC.

2. The cost to start investing in mutual funds is lower than for other types of investments.

3. There are fees associated with buying and redeeming mutual funds. In addition, every fund has account maintenance fees and other costs and fees, regardless of how the fund performs. It's important to consider these fees before investing. Excluding the fees associated with buying or redeeming fund shares, the *expense radio* given in the *prospectus* lists the fund's costs calculated as a percentage to the total assets of the fund. Even *no-load funds* have an expense ratio—fees for which you'll be responsible, directly or indirectly.

4. A fund's NAV is calculated by adding up the current values of its holdings, subtracting the manager's salary and the operating expenses, and then dividing that figure by the fund's total number of shares.

5. A mutual fund's NAV is calculated once daily, at the end of the business day, after the stock exchanges have closed. When you buy or redeem shares of a mutual fund, the price you pay or receive is based on that day's NAV, which won't be calculated until that evening.

6. You should always read a fund's prospectus and shareholder report carefully and then determine how the fund has performed in the past, how risky it has been, what it owns, who the fund manager is, and what costs and fees are associated with the fund. Answers to these questions will provide you with a better idea of the fund and whether or not you should add it to your investment portfolio. You can also look at the rating a fund receives from a respected, independent third-party source, such as Morningstar.

7. With little effort and minimal time, you can get from the right mutual fund investments a *return on investment* (ROI) that's significantly higher than you would get from putting your money in a traditional savings account at a bank.

8. Mutual funds can hold stocks, bonds, and/or other securities. There are three categories of mutual funds—money market funds, bonds funds, and stock funds. Chapter 4 offers more detail on types of funds. From this book, you'll also learn about *exchange-traded funds* (ETFs), which are somewhat similar to mutual funds in terms of their appeal to investors.

9. The past performance of a mutual fund is in no way an indicator of how it will perform in the future.

10. Shares in a mutual fund are purchased from the fund itself (or through a broker who represents the fund). In contrast, stock shares are purchased through a stock exchange, such as the New York Stock Exchange or the NASDAQ Stock Exchange.

Mutual Fund Key Term

SHAREHOLDER REPORT A document created by the mutual fund company for its shareholders that reveals fund performance and discloses information about the fund's holdings, investment strategies, expenses, and other details of interest to shareholders. This report can be issued annually, semiannually, or quarterly. You'll find more information about this important document within Chapter 4.

NO-LOAD FUND A mutual fund that does not charge a sales commission (*load*) when an investor purchases shares. However, no-load funds have operating expenses and charge other fees.

Types of People Who Invest in Mutual Funds

One of the great things about mutual funds is that virtually anyone can start investing in them, with a relatively low initial investment. Once you do your research and pick your funds, setting up an account and buying into a fund takes less than 30 minutes. The process can be done over the telephone, online, by mail, or in person. How this is done will be explained in Chapter 6.

While it's essential to do research and understand how mutual funds work, once you've developed an investment strategy, it takes just a few minutes to periodically review

Investing Tip

ANYONE CAN INVEST To invest in mutual funds, you don't need a college education, a high income, or a lot of money to invest initially. You also don't have to put a lot of time into managing your portfolio or take on any more risk than you're comfortable with.

your portfolio, see how it's performing, and then make adjustments as needed in order to better achieve your long-term investment objectives.

Since mutual funds are readily available to just about everyone with even a little bit of money to invest, they have become popular with people of all ages and from all walks of life. As you learn more about the opportunities mutual funds offer, you too will most likely see how you can benefit from using this type of investment to help you achieve your long-term financial goals.

Why People Invest in Mutual Funds

People invest in mutual funds for many reasons, depending on their financial goals. This section covers just some of the common reasons.

Build wealth and security. For many people, investing in mutual funds is a way to increase their savings and establish financial security. The returns from mutual funds are often higher than what could be earned from a traditional bank savings account. The risk is also much lower than with other types of investments.

Buy a home or another big-ticket item. If you're saving up for a down payment on a home or another big-ticket item, investing in mutual funds can help that money grow faster, without much risk.

Money Saver

MORE RESOURCES If you're a first-time homebuyer or planning to become one, pick up a copy of *Entrepreneur Magazine's Pocket Guide—Why Rent? Own Your Dream Home* or *Entrepreneur Magazine's Pocket Guide—Mortgages and Refinancing: Get the Best Rates,* available wherever personal finance books are sold. Visit *www.entrepreneurpress.com* for information about other books in this series.

Give to charity. Some people invest in mutual funds and then donate all dividends and capital gains from their investments to charities. In many cases, charitable donations are tax-deductible. Your accountant or financial planner can help you develop an investment plan suitable for making charitable donations on an ongoing basis.

Create an emergency fund. Most financial advisors encourage their clients to create an emergency fund that can cover all living expenses for three to six months, in the event their clients lose their jobs, get injured, become ill, or are unable to work for other reasons. This fund could also be used to pay for emergency home or auto repairs or unexpected medical bills, for example. Investing in a low-risk, highly liquid mutual fund can be an excellent way to establish, build, and maintain an emergency fund.

Estate planning. Certain types of mutual fund investments can be used for estate-planning purposes to help ensure that your loved ones (the beneficiaries of your estate) will receive the most money possible after your passing. Your accountant or financial planner can help you choose the right investment strategy for this goal.

Retirement. Without a doubt, the most common reason why people invest in mutual funds is to save for their retirement. There is a wide range of funds with long-term investment strategies that take full advantage of the favorable tax laws associated with saving and investing for retirement. The earlier in life you begin saving for retirement, the better off you'll be. Your accountant, financial planner, or investment advisor can help you develop a solid investment strategy for your retirement. The money you invest in mutual funds associated with saving for your retirement is tax-deferred. This can save you hundreds, even thousands of dollars per year.

Saving for college. The cost of higher education continues to go higher and higher. The more money you can save for education, the less you'll need in student loans and the less interest you'll pay on those loans. Using mutual funds to save can be an excellent strategy. Your financial planner or investment advisor can help you develop an investment plan, based on how much time you have before the education bills begin.

Upcoming life events. Some people use mutual fund investments to create a nest egg, knowing that in the future they'll need to cover significant expenses related to life. For example, if you're planning to start a family and have kids, start a business, or pay for an extravagant wedding, proper planning and using the most suitable mutual fund investment opportunities can help ensure that you'll have the money you'll need, whether the life event is five, ten, or 20 years in the future.

No matter what your eventual needs for money, by properly investing money now and through time, in mutual funds and in other investment opportunities, you should be able to achieve your long-term financial goals. It's important, however, that your goals be realistic and that you take the steps necessary to make intelligent and well-thought-out investment decisions—starting immediately.

Reasons to Start Investing Right Now

Because of the diversification associated with mutual funds, your decision about investing in mutual funds should not be affected whatsoever by the current state of the economy or where you think the economy is headed. Mutual fund investing is not a "get-rich-quick" scheme. With mutual funds, it will most likely take you many months, perhaps years or decades, depending on the types of funds, to achieve significant returns.

While you could potentially get rich very quickly by investing in individual stocks and other types of securities, the risk involved with these types of investments, the knowledge required, and the time commitment necessary to manage those investments are usually too significant for the average person.

After reading the previous section, perhaps you've already pinpointed one, two, or three areas of your life where mutual fund investments will be able to help you achieve your financial goals. To do so, however, you must take the steps necessary to start planning and then to invest.

For example, to ensure that you'll have ample money available for retirement, many financial planners recommend saving five percent of your income annually, starting when you're in your early to mid-20s. If you wait until your 30s to start saving, you will most likely need to invest at least 10 to 15 percent of your income annually. The longer you wait, the larger the percentage of your income needed to ensure enough money by the time you retire.

If you have long-term financial goals, but haven't yet made plans to achieve those goals, there's no better time than the present to start. Once you learn more about mutual funds, by reading this book and using some of the resources mentioned, hopefully you'll discover how easy it can be to invest successfully.

Before you start investing, however, you must set short-term and long-term financial goals. You should base those goals on your current financial situation and the amounts you'll want or need in the future. The next chapter will help you develop realistic goals.

Mutual Funds Can Be Fun and Exciting

Many people discover that learning how to invest in mutual funds and then establishing an investment portfolio can be a fun, exciting, and rewarding experience. In fact, there are investment clubs throughout the country that provide both educational opportunities and social outlets for investors.

Appendix A offers information about additional resources you can use to learn more about mutual funds and other investment opportunities. As you'll see, there is an abundance of investing-related Web sites, magazines, books, newsletters, radio shows, television programs, blogs, podcasts, classes, and seminars. There are also countless online tools (many of which are described in this book and cost nothing) that make managing your mutual fund investment portfolio a simple and stress-free experience that requires a minimal time commitment on your part.

Investing Tip

AN ENJOYABLE EXPERIENCE One way to increase the enjoyment you receive from investing is to seek out investments that interest you (and that make sense, based on your goals). In terms of mutual funds, for example, there are many funds that focus on specific industries, such as media, telecommunications, health care, finance, consumer goods, energy, utilities, or manufacturing. Some funds also have narrow focuses and pursue very specific types of investments. Other funds rally around a cause, such as investing primarily in environmentally friendly companies.

CHAPTER 2

Defining Your Investment Goals

WHAT'S IN THIS CHAPTER

- Analyzing your current financial situation
- Defining your short-term and long-term goals
- Deciding how much risk you're willing to accept
- Gathering the money you'll need to start investing

Before you contemplate making investments and start putting your money to work for you, you must first determine specifically *why* you're investing and what you hope to gain from your investments. In other words, what are your goals? Next, you must analyze your current financial situation to determine whether investing in mutual funds and/or other investment opportunities is worthwhile at this point in your life. You may discover that it's better to first pay off some of your high-interest debts and loans.

If you're currently paying off credit card balances, a car loan, a mortgage, student loans, and/or other significant debts, the interest and fees you're paying each month on those loans could be in the hundreds or thousands of dollars.

In many situations, it makes more financial sense to pay off your high-interest debts *before* starting an investment portfolio for any other reason than retirement. It usually makes financial sense to invest money for your retirement, starting as early in your adult life as possible. Mutual funds can be an excellent investment for retirement.

If you determine that you can manage your current debt and it makes sense for you to invest some of your discretionary income in mutual funds, the next decision is how much risk you're willing to accept with your investments.

The main focus of this chapter is to get you ready to start investing, by focusing on developing your short- and long-term goals, evaluating your current financial situation, and determining how much risk you're willing to accept.

Then, you'll be ready to take the next step, which is to start researching potential mutual fund investment opportunities.

Analyze Your Current Financial Situation

Creating an investment portfolio is something you can (and probably should) do with some of your *discretionary income*. This is money that's left over, after you've paid all of your monthly living expenses. You'll probably want to use some of your discretionary income to purchase items you want, as opposed to what you need, such as a new pair of shoes, items for your home, new golf clubs, or a vacation. However, if you regularly and systematically take a portion of your discretionary income and invest it, you'll create a financial nest egg that can grow through the years.

> **DISCRETIONARY INCOME** The money remaining after paying all monthly bills, expenses, and taxes.
>
>
>
> **Mutual Fund Key Term**

Before investing your discretionary income, however, you'll probably want to pay off your high-interest debts. Let's begin by looking at your current personal financial situation.

To begin analyzing your current financial situation, gather your recent pay stubs or copies of recent paychecks, your checking and savings account statements, and your bills from the past three months or so. Use the information from these documents to complete the following financial worksheets.

Investment Tip

PAYING YOURSELF Among the payments that you make every month should be one to your retirement account. Your financial planner, accountant, or investment advisor can help you develop a personalized plan for investing for retirement using tax-deferred investments, including mutual funds. Depending on your age, income, and net worth, it's typically smart to invest five to 15 percent of your monthly income for retirement.

Financial Worksheets

Monthly Income

Income	Dollars
Current Salary (including any tips, commissions, and bonuses)	$
Other Sources of Income (such as interest, alimony, child support, investment dividends, etc.)	$
Total Average Monthly Income	$

Total Savings

Savings	Dollars
Checking Account Balance(s)	$
Investments (stocks, mutual funds, etc.)	$
Retirement Fund Contribution(s)	$
Savings Account Balance(s)	$
Other Savings	$
Total Savings:	$

Mutual Funds: A Quick-Start Guide

Total Monthly Expenses

Monthly Expenses	Dollars
Alimony	$
Car Expenses (monthly car payments, gas, repairs, insurance, etc.)	$
Child Support	$
Clothing	$
Entertainment	$
Food	$
Insurance (health insurance, car insurance, life insurance, renter's insurance, etc.)	$
Investment in IRA, Keogh, 401(k), or other retirement plans	$
Medical Expenses	$
Rent/Mortgage	$
Taxes (federal and state income taxes, real estate taxes, etc.)	$
Utilities (electricity, gas, telephone, cell phone, Internet, etc.)	$
Other Expenses	$
Total Monthly Expenses:	**$**

Current Debt and Debt-Related Expenses

Monthly Expenses	Monthly Payment ($)	Interest Rate (%)	Outstanding Balance ($)
Car Loan(s)	$	$	$
Monthly Child Support Payment(s)	$	$	$
Credit Card(s)	$	$	$
Outstanding Medical Bills	$	$	$
School/Education Loans	$	$	$
Mortgage	$	$	$
Other Debt	$	$	$
Total Monthly Debt and Debt-Related Expenses:	$	$	$

These financial worksheets can help you figure out exactly how you're using your money. To calculate your discretionary income, take your monthly income and subtract your monthly expenses and what you spend every month paying off debt.

Monthly Income – Monthly Expenses – Debt-Related Expenses = Discretionary Income

If you determine that your discretionary income is a negative number, then you're spending more than you're earning every month. As a result, you're either adding debt every month or tapping into your savings. In either case, this is a bad situation that you should improve as soon as possible in order to avoid financial problems.

If you're spending more than you're earning, don't even consider investing in mutual funds (or any other investments) until you have your budget under control. There are many strategies for cutting costs that you can adopt either on your own or with the help of your accountant or financial planner. Ideally, you should invest the time and effort needed to create and follow a strict monthly budget that will allow you to live within your financial means, hopefully without impacting your quality of life too much. Relying on credit cards or your savings to cover your monthly living expenses is a strategy that'll lead to serious financial problems, usually sooner than later.

Investing Tip

MORE INFORMATION To learn more about managing your debt, creating a personal budget, and living within your financial means, pick up a copy of *Smart Debt*, published by Entrepreneur Press. It's available from bookstores everywhere or from *www.EntrepreneurPress.com*.

Now, let's take a look at your current debt and your debt-related expenses. It's important to figure out how much you're paying each month in interest and other fees that are directly related to your debt. This is money you're forced to spend every month that you could put to much better use once you pay off your debt.

Many people have mortgages and car loans. If you're one of them, there are ways to minimize the financial burden of these debts. For example, you could refinance your mortgage to lower your monthly payment and interest rate. For your other debts, there are strategies that could reduce the amount you pay each month on interest and fees, depending on your *credit score* and credit history (your past relationship with lenders and creditors and your record for paying). For example, you could transfer your high-interest credit card balances to credit cards with lower interest rates. You could also consolidate your credit card bills and other debts into a single, lower-interest loan.

Mutual Fund Key Term

CREDIT SCORE A three-digit number between 300 and 850 that is calculated based on your credit (financial) reputation and history with creditors. Using a complex formula and many criteria related to your current financial situation and credit history, the three major credit reporting agencies calculate and regularly update your credit score.

How important is your credit score? According to the Federal Trade Commission, "Most creditors use credit scoring to evaluate your credit record. This involves using your credit application and report to get information about you, such as your annual income, outstanding debt, bill paying history, and the number and types of accounts you have and how long you have had them. Potential lenders use your credit score to help predict whether you are a good risk to repay a loan and make payments on time."

Your immediate financial goal should probably be to pay off your high-interest debts. But, while you're doing this, take steps to ensure that you're paying the lowest interest rates and fees you qualify for. If you find yourself with extensive debt (a situation all too common among Americans), seek the help of an accountant or financial planner to find ways to lower your monthly debt-related expenses.

If you're paying an annual percentage rate (APR) of 10, 20, or even 30 percent on your credit cards, plus raking up a wide range of credit card-related fees, but only paying the minimum requirement payment on each card, this can not only damage your credit score (a measure of your credit worthiness calculated by the credit bureaus), it can also keep you from achieving your long-term financial goals. Using this strategy, it will take you many years to totally pay off your credit card debt.

ANNUAL PERCENTAGE RATE (APR) A measure of the cost of credit, expressed as a yearly interest rate. All loans and forms of credit that charge interest have an APR.	 **Mutual Fund Key Term**

By adopting a few strategies for lowering your debt, you'll save a fortune in interest charges and fees over time, pay off your debt much faster, and be able to use much more of your income for better purposes. By increasing your discretionary income, you'll have more money to invest, to put to work for you.

Even if your financial position is relatively strong, you can still adopt basic strategies for decreasing your debt-related expenses, so you'll have more discretionary income to invest. If you have discretionary income each month, you can spend that money on items to improve your quality of life right now—or you can invest some or all of that money to build your net worth and to earn more money.

Investing Tip

KNOW YOUR BRACKET Because your mutual fund investments should generate a return, which will be taxable income, you should know your current tax bracket and then determine whether the additional income will put you in a higher tax bracket and increase the tax you'll owe to the state and federal governments. There are tax-free mutual fund investment opportunities that might serve you well—and will not affect your tax bracket. If you're in a high tax bracket now, the additional income from your investments most likely will have little effect on your tax rate.

Calculate How Much Money You Can Use to Start Investing

If your financial situation is good right now and you have money to establish an investment portfolio, you should look at your completed Total Savings Worksheet. How much money do you have now in a savings account at a bank or another type of low-interest account? If you won't need this money for at least six to 12 months, you could potentially use it to establish your investment portfolio.

Next, look at your monthly discretionary income. Could you afford to invest $100, $200, $500, or more a month, every

Investing Tip

MINIMUM INVESTMENT To start investing in mutual funds and buy into a fund, you'll typically need an initial investment of at least $2,500, unless you're creating a retirement account. Then, most funds allow you to invest as little as $50 at a time (maybe even less).

month? If so, establishing an *automatic investment plan* is extremely smart for reasons that we'll explore later. Investing even $100 a month in a mutual fund that's generating good returns can dramatically increase the value of your portfolio and your net worth over time.

Take a look at the financial calculations you've done as you've completed the financial worksheets in this chapter. From these worksheets, you should be able to easily determine if you're in a financial position right now to start investing and, if so, how much you can invest to establish your portfolio. Depending on how much you have available to start investing, you might want to find just one or two mutual funds for now and then consider diversifying later. This is a sound strategy for beginners, because the holdings of any mutual fund are already diversified, so the risk you're taking with your money is typically lower than if you were to invest in another type of security, such as an individual stock. ·

Define Your Short-Term and Long-Term Goals

If you haven't done so already, figure out your short-term and long-term personal, professional, and financial goals. Once you know what you're trying to get out of life, you can adopt strategies to achieve each of your goals.

If you know what your life goals are, you can create financial goals. Once you know what your financial goals are and understand the time frame in which you hope to achieve them (your time horizon), you can more easily identify appropriate mutual funds and other investment opportunities. The following checklist will help you set some goals that will impact your finances and determine how quickly you'll need to have large sums of money to pay for significant expenses.

Potential Goal (What you'll need a large sum of money for in the future)	Within 1 to 5 Years	Wtihin 6 to 10 Years	10+ Years
Buy a boat	❑	❑	❑
Buy a home	❑	❑	❑
Buy a car	❑	❑	❑
Buy a second home	❑	❑	❑
Get married	❑	❑	❑
Major appliance purchase	❑	❑	❑
Major home repair or improvement	❑	❑	❑
Pay for school (college) tuition	❑	❑	❑
Retirement	❑	❑	❑
Start a family (new children)	❑	❑	❑
Vacation	❑	❑	❑
Get divorced, then pay a one-time settlement or alimony payment(s)	❑	❑	❑
Other goals	❑	❑	❑

By saving or investing to acquire money you'll need to achieve your goals, you can avoid the need to take out large loans or use high-interest credit cards. This will save you a fortune in interest charges and fees. For example, if you know you'll need $25,000 for a flashy new car in three to five years, you can invest a specific amount of money each month in the right type of mutual fund and slowly build up enough money to pay for that car outright or at least make a significant down payment so you can borrow less money and thus pay less in interest.

With proper planning, as far in advance as possible, you can create strategies for saving significant amounts of money with relative ease, without impacting your standard of living. Mutual funds are an easy and low-risk way to make your money grow and work better for you.

Once you set your goals and decide how you'll want and need to spend your money in the future, the next step is to prioritize those goals and focus on the ones that are most important. Figure out which goals you'll need to achieve first in order. Regardless of your other financial goals, investing for your retirement should take priority. This not only offers significant tax advantages but also helps to prepare you for your future.

Warning

INVEST ENOUGH TO MAKE YOUR GOALS Your financial and investment goals must be realistic. If you know you'll need $25,000 in three years, investing just $100 per month, even in the most aggressive and highly rated mutual funds, isn't going to generate the return on investment you want or need. However, that $100-per-month investment can grow significantly over ten to 20 years, for example. Also, you should not consider mutual funds your sole, "perfect solution" for achieving all of your financial goals. Mutual funds should be one part of a comprehensive and well-thought-out, long-term spending, saving, and investment strategy.

Investing Tip

KNOW YOUR TIME HORIZON If your financial goals will require you to use your money within two or three years, consider investing in money market or short-term bond funds. If your needs are more like seven, ten, or 20 years away, stock funds will most likely be a more suitable investment.

Goal Worksheet

Setting definite goals will help you determine what you'll need money for, how much money you'll need, and when you'll need it. So, start by listing your personal and professional goals for the short term (within the next six months to one year) and the long term (beyond one year).

For every goal you set, it's essential to understand specifically how you will benefit from achieving it. Also, for each goal, you'll want to develop a step-by-step plan for achieving it. If a goal is large, you could develop a timeline of smaller goals and set a deadline for each. By determining strategies and setting deadlines, you'll create a map or a guide that can help keep you on track and working toward your objectives.

Once you've set your goals and begun implementing plans for achieving each of them, keep a diary or detailed records of your progress—from day to day, month to month, or year to year, depending on the goal. If you're able to measure the progress you're making toward each goal and document it and if you're excited about the benefit(s) you'll receive from achieving each goal, you'll find it much easier to stay focused and motivated.

You might also want to list obstacles you may encounter as you work toward each goal and then plan ways to overcome those obstacles. If you know what to expect and have a plan for dealing with potential problems, you'll experience far less stress and difficulty along the way.

Expect challenges and know that hard work, persistence, and dedication will be necessary to achieve your goals. Of course, as time goes on, you'll find that your goals will change or evolve. Thus, every six months, sit down and review your goals, then tweak them as needed to account for changes that have occurred in your life as well as any new directions your life has taken. Developing a detailed plan will help you decide how to invest, based on your needs, wants, expectations, goals, and time horizons.

Personal Goals. Here are some examples of short-term personal goals:

- Buy a new car
- Buy a new computer
- Buy a new wardrobe
- Go on dates and find a new boyfriend or girlfriend
- Lose weight
- Quit smoking
- Redecorate your home
- Take a vacation
- Take some adult education classes

Here are examples of long-term personal goals:

- Return to school to earn a master's degree or a doctorate
- Buy a new sports car
- Get married and start a family
- Buy a home

For each of your short-term personal goals, write down the goal and then briefly describe your plan for achieving it. Finally, set a realistic timeline or deadline for each goal.

Short-Term Personal Goals

Goal Description	Plan for Achieving the Goal	Timeframe or Deadline

Long-Term Personal Goals

Goal Description	Plan for Achieving the Goal	Timeframe or Deadline

Professional Goals. Here are examples of short-term professional goals:

- Earn a raise or promotion within the next six months
- Take classes that will improve your professional skills and your earning potential
- Revise your resume and start looking for a better-paying and more enjoyable job

Here are examples of long-term professional goals:

- Become a senior vice president at your company within the next five years
- Start a business
- Retire by age 55

Short-Term Professional Goals

Goal Description	Plan for Achieving the Goal	Timeframe or Deadline

Long-Term Professional Goals

Goal Description	Plan for Achieving the Goal	Timeframe or Deadline

Financial Goals. Your financial goals should relate directly to your personal or professional goals, since you'll probably need money to achieve those goals. Plus, your professional goals will most likely determine how much money you earn.

The financial goals you set could have to do with how you earn and/or spend your money, how you're planning to invest, how you'll manage your money and/or investments, or how you'll pay off debts or loans.

You'll probably discover that your personal goals and professional goals will all somehow relate to your financial goals. For example, if you're planning to buy a home in the next five to seven years, you'll need to develop a financial plan for coming up with the down payment. Once you know what your financial goals are, you can either do research or sit down with a financial planner, accountant, or investment advisor for help putting together a systematic plan for achieving them.

Short-Term Financial Goals

Goal Description	Plan for Achieving the Goal	Timeframe or Deadline

Long-Term Financial Goals

Goal Description	Plan for Achieving the Goal	Timeframe or Deadline

Decide How Much Risk You're Willing to Accept

When you deposit money into your savings or checking account at a bank, that money is secure. It's insured by the FDIC. And you'll probably earn a little interest on that money (at least in your savings account).

While your money can sit safely for an indefinite time in a savings or checking account at your bank, that money isn't really growing or working for you. It's just being stored more safely than under your mattress. One of the reasons why so many people invest in mutual funds is because these investments generally provide a significantly higher rate of return than a basic savings account. So, instead of earning one to three percent interest, you could achieve a return on investment of five, ten, 15, 20, or 30 percent or more over time, by investing in the right mutual fund(s).

This sounds good, right? Well, there's a catch! The money you invest in mutual funds is *not* insured. Thus, you run the risk that your investment will lose money. It's virtually impossible to lose your entire investment when you invest in a mutual fund. However, the value could drop significantly, especially in the short term, due mainly to volatility in the market.

VOLATILITY In investing, the degree to which the value of an investment fluctuates, from hour to hour, day to day, week to week, month to month, or year to year. The value of an extremely volatile stock or mutual fund can go up and down quickly, often, and sometimes unexpectedly.

Mutual Fund Key Term

How much risk you assume when investing in a mutual fund depends on the type of fund, its holdings, its level of diversification, the investment strategies utilized by the fund's manager, and various other factors. As you'll learn in Chapters 4 and 5, individual mutual funds can be analyzed

Warning

RISK AND RETURN A fund that generates a high rate of return typically achieves this return by taking on significant risk. As a general rule for many types of investments, the greater the risk, the greater the potential reward. Many stocks, for example, are extremely volatile: their value can rise and fall, sometimes dramatically. If a mutual fund's holdings are primarily volatile stocks, you can expect the fund's NAV to rise and fall. Many investment advisors recommend that investors avoid putting *all* of their money into individual stocks or stock funds, because of this volatility and uncertainty.

and ranked based on their risk. There are many types of very low-risk funds, just as there are funds that are ranked as extremely risky.

Investing Tip

DIVERSIFY DIVERSITY Diversification is one of the best ways an investor can reduce overall risk. While you may opt to put all of your investment money into mutual funds, which can be a sound strategy because the holdings of a specific mutual fund are already somewhat diversified, you'll probably want to diversify your portfolio of funds by buying into a combination of money market funds, bond funds, and stock funds. You can further reduce your risk by buying into funds that invest primarily in U.S.-based securities and others that have an international focus.

The level of risk you're willing to accept should be based on several factors, including the following:

- The amount of time you plan to keep the money invested.
- Your ability to handle the emotional implications of making risky investments. Will you experience stress, heartburn, or an emotional breakdown, for example, every time you see a negative fluctuation in your portfolio's value?
- Your financial goals with respect to the expectations you have for the investment's performance.
- Your financial stability and the impact a decline in your portfolio's value would have on your overall financial health.

There are several kinds of risk in investing. One is *market risk*. This represents how your investments will perform when the market as a whole goes up or down. If a mutual fund focuses on investing within a specific industry or sector, any hardships in that industry or sector will impact that fund.

If stocks in a particular mutual fund's portfolio are over-valued and experience a sudden drop, if the fund is not adequately diversified to handle fluctuations in the market, or if the funds you invest in don't achieve returns that at least keep up with inflation or don't meet your long-term expectations—these also are risks to consider.

In Chapter 5, you'll learn about risk analysis tools from companies like Morningstar that you can use to measure the risk of a mutual fund or your portfolio as a whole.

Investing Tip

LOOK FOR LOW FEES Another strategy for reducing some of your risk with mutual funds is to seek out funds with low fees and costs. The fees and costs associated with mutual funds are money that you must recoup before you break even or generate a profit from your investment. The higher the fees and costs, the better the fund must perform.

No matter how much money you'll ultimately be investing or what types of mutual funds or other investment opportunities you'll pursue, part of your initial research should be to help determine the level of risk associated with the investment. You must then decide whether or not you can accept that level of risk, based on your personality, circumstances, and overall investment strategies.

Gather Your Funds to Get Started Investing

Now that you've completed the Financial Worksheets in this chapter, you've set goals for yourself, and you've begun thinking about how much risk you're willing to accept when making investments, you're almost ready to begin establishing your investment portfolio and researching specific mutual funds.

You should also know how much money you have available right now to invest. Keep in mind that you'll typically need to make an initial investment of at least $2,500 per mutual fund, unless you're investing for retirement. Also, based on your financial situation, will you be able to find at least $100 per month in your budget to invest using an automatic investment plan? Participating in this type of plan will force you to make regular contributions to your portfolio, which is one strategy for building long-term wealth.

The next chapter focuses on finding a reliable and knowledgeable investment advisor and the investment help you'll need as you get started.

Getting the Investment Help You Need

WHAT'S IN THIS CHAPTER

- Advice for selecting an investment advisor
- Understanding an investment advisor's credentials
- The fees you'll pay for the help you'll want and need
- An interview with a Certified Financial Planner (CFP)

To invest in stocks and many other types of securities, an investor works through a *broker*—an intermediary who is licensed to buy and sell securities through the stock exchanges. In addition, a broker often offers investment advice and portfolio management services to clients. The broker receives a fee for these services.

Mutual funds are *not* traded through stock exchanges. Thus, mutual fund investors need not work with a broker. However, if you'll be investing in *exchange-traded funds* (ETFs), which are described in Chapter 4, you will need to work through a broker.

Mutual fund investors can invest directly with the company that manages the mutual fund(s) they choose to buy into. Most mutual fund companies offer investors easy ways to invest online, by telephone, in person, or by mail. Many of these companies, like Fidelity Investments, Charles Schwab, T. Rowe Price, and Vanguard, just to name a few, also have large staffs of experts who can offer free guidance and they provide a wide range of tools investors can use in choosing the most appropriate mutual funds.

Investing Tip

ONE-STOP SHOPS Companies like Fidelity Investments and T. Rowe Price, for example, are one-stop shops designed to meet all of your investing needs. These companies manage a wide range of mutual funds, but also offer brokerage and other investment services. It's important to choose a company that has a good reputation and that offers the services and support you want and need.

If you need or want investment advice, instead of turning to a broker you can use the services of an *investment advisor*. Investment advisors are experts who can help you identify your needs and select investments suitable to your financial goals. They can also offer advice on managing your entire investment portfolio. You will typically pay a fee for these services.

CERTIFIED FINANCIAL PLANNER (CFP) A financial planning expert who has been credentialed by the Certified Financial Planner Board of Standards. Not all financial planners are "certified." Only those people who have fulfilled the requirements of the CFP Board can use the CFP certification mark: they must complete the required education, pass a comprehensive certification exam, have a minimum of three years' experience as a financial planner, and adhere to the strict code of ethics mandated by the CFP Board. A CFP can serve as an investment or financial advisor, a money manager, or a portfolio manager, depending on his or her area of expertise. For more information, visit the CFP Board's Web site (*www.cfp.net*).

Mutual Fund Key Term

Plenty of mutual fund investors opt to do research themselves and are comfortable managing their own investment portfolios, without using the services of an investment advisor. For these people, there are free or relatively inexpensive analytical and portfolio management tools to help casual, moderate, and even serious investors. Many companies, such as Fidelity Investments, Charles Schwab, T. Rowe Price and Vanguard, offer free personalized advice from investment advisors. In most cases, these people are paid a salary, not a

Investing Tip

THE VALUE OF INDEPENDENCE Hiring an independent and unbiased investment advisor will cost you money, in addition to the fees involved with buying, owning, and selling mutual fund shares (and other types of securities). Many investors opt to make all of their investing decisions alone and manage their portfolios themselves or use the free services offered by many mutual fund companies.

commission based on the advice offered or investment products endorsed. (Make sure this is the case with the company or individuals you opt to work with.)

This chapter will help you determine if and when you need the services of an investment advisor and offers strategies for finding the best expert for your specific needs. At the end of this chapter, you'll read an exclusive, in-depth interview with Stuart Ritter, a Certified Financial Planner and mutual fund expert employed by T. Rowe Price.

Who Needs an Investment Advisor?

Investment advisors are typically experts in their field, but they're not psychics. Nobody can predict with 100 percent accuracy how the market will perform or which mutual funds or other investment opportunities will rise in value. Investment advisors know how to help people set their financial and investing goals. They typically have a thorough knowledge of the investment opportunities available and expertise using a wide range of analytical and research tools.

Some people use an investment advisor exclusively to help them establish their investment portfolio. Other people develop a long-term relationship with their investment advisor, which can last for decades. Your decision to use an investment advisor or not should be based on several criteria, including the following:

- How much money you'll be investing and the size of your portfolio
- How much time and effort you want to devote to researching investment opportunities and managing your portfolio
- Whether or not you're willing to pay the fees associated with hiring an independent investment advisor
- What your long-term financial goals are
- How comfortable you are making your own investment decisions and managing your portfolio
- Whether your portfolio will be composed of just mutual funds or will also include individual stocks and other types of securities

Investing Tip

BEING PASSIVE People who pay an independent investment advisor to manage their portfolio tend to have a high net worth and long-term investment goals who choose to take a passive role in managing their portfolio. If you choose this course, keep in mind that "passive" does not mean *absentee*.

Selecting Your Investment Advisor

Regardless of whom you decide to use as your investment advisor, here are a few traits you'll definitely want:

You want someone who is trustworthy and with whom you can communicate openly and honestly about your personal finances. It's essential that your investment advisor understand your financial situation and goals, so you must fully disclose detailed information about your finances.

You want someone who is experienced and well-trained. You want to receive advice that is appropriate to your needs and that you can trust.

You want to be comfortable with the investment style, philosophies, and strategies of your investment advisor. This includes being comfortable with the level of risk you're taking on with your investments.

The relationship between you and your advisor should be well documented. You want and need to know what services you can expect, when you should expect to receive them, and how much they'll cost. For example, you should know how

Investing Tip

When you use an investment advisor to manage your portfolio, you can give him or her the power to handle all investment-related decisions. However, it remains your responsibility to keep track of how your portfolio is performing and what your advisor is doing. Make sure your advisor adheres to the investment plan and strategies to which you agree, which should be put in writing.

often you'll be meeting with your financial advisor, what written reports you'll receive, and what information those reports will contain about the status of your portfolio.

The term "investment advisor" has become a generic title used by anyone who advises others on investing their money. Most competent investment advisors will possess one or more certifications or accreditations.

The very best way to find an investment advisor is through a referral from someone you know and trust, who has achieved good results through the advisor he or she is recommending. You might also be able to find an independent investment advisor through your bank, the Yellow Pages, the Internet, or a referral from a professional trade association. Chances are, your mutual fund company will have highly skilled investment advisors on staff and available to you either in person or by telephone.

The ABCs of CFAs, CFPs, CPAs, ChFCs, and RIAs

As you begin your quest to find an investment advisor, you'll come across people with different combinations of accreditations and certifications. Here are some of the popular accreditations and certifications and what they mean:

Certified Financial Analyst (CFA). This is a professional designation awarded by the CFA Institute (*www.cfainstitute.org*). It measures the competence and integrity of financial analysts. To obtain this accreditation, a person must have at least three years of work experience and pass three levels of exams covering areas such as accounting, economics, ethics, money management, and security analysis.

Certified Financial Planner (CFP). Someone who has obtained specialized training and meets the strict guidelines of the Certified Financial Planner Board of Standards (*www.cfp.net*) can earn the right to use this certification mark. Many investment advisors employed by the mutual fund companies and who offer advice to clients are CFPs.

Certified Public Accountant (CPA). This is a designation that an accountant can earn through the American Institute of Certified Public Accountants (*www.aicpa.org*), by passing a specific exam, meeting a variety of other work experience and related requirements, and adhering to a strict code of ethics.

Chartered Financial Consultant (ChFC). This designation from The American College (*www.theamericancollege.edu*) shows that the financial planner has successfully completed courses in financial planning, investments, insurance planning, income taxation, retirement planning, and estate planning. To date, more than 41,000 financial professionals have earned this certification.

Registered Investment Advisor (RIA). This is an investment advisor who is registered with the Securities and Exchange Commission (SEC), which is generally a requirement when managing over $25 million in investments. Investment advisors who manage less than $25 million register with the securities regulatory agency in the state(s) in which they do business. RIAs typically earn their revenue through a management fee, which is calculated based on a percentage of assets managed for a client. Fees vary; the average is around one percent of the value of the client's portfolio.

Because you'll be entrusting your money with your investment advisor, it's essential to choose the right person. Your choice should be based on the following factors, in addition to a positive referral:

- Education
- Experience
- Investment philosophies
- Personality
- Professional credentials
- Qualifications
- Track record
- Trustworthiness and integrity

When you meet with potential investment advisors for the first time, they should provide you with reasonably detailed information about themselves, their credentials and/or certifications, their services, their fees, their investment philosophies, their experience, and information about the company they work for or represent (if applicable). They should be willing to discuss your personal needs, offer details about how they would address those needs, and be willing to patiently give straightforward and detailed answers to all of your questions. Ideally, at least your initial meeting should be in person, but this isn't absolutely necessary.

Investment advisors should be upfront and honest about how they are compensated, especially if they receive commissions for recommending or selling specific investment products or specific funds or if they are affiliated with a specific company.

Questions to Ask a Potential Investment Advisor

To get the information you'll want and need before choosing an investment advisor, be prepared to ask a lot of questions during your initial meeting. These questions also apply when hiring a broker.

Warning

The answers you receive to your questions should be honest, straightforward, and accurate. If you're not comfortable with the answers, seek out someone else. It's essential that you trust the investment advisor you hire. He or she must be willing to answer your questions and address your concerns. You should feel very confident about his or her capabilities.

Here are some questions you might ask an investment advisor:

- What experience do you have in the investment industry?
- How long have you been working as an investment advisor?
- How many clients do you currently represent?
- In total, how much money do you currently invest or manage for your clients?

- What is your educational background?
- What professional credentials and accreditations do you possess?
- Are you an active member of any professional organizations?
- What states are you registered or licensed to work in? Are you registered with the SEC?
- Have you ever been sued by a client? If so, what was the reason and what was the outcome?
- What services do you offer to your clients?
- Do you personally work with all of your clients or do you have a staff?
- What are your fees? Are you compensated exclusively through fees, fees and commissions, salary, or commissions only? If you're paid commissions, what is the commission rate for each recommended financial product?
- Based on my financial goals and initial investment, what would your investment strategy be?
- How would you diversity my portfolio?
- What types of written reports would I receive as a client? What information would they contain? How often do you provide the reports?
- Do you fully understand my investment and financial goals, as well as my tolerance for risk?

As you initially interact with an investment advisor, determine whether you feel a sense of chemistry with this person. Is he or she explaining complex or important concepts in ways you can easily understand? If you're looking to establish a long-term relationship with the investment advisor, do you believe he or she will still be around in five, ten, or 15 years? Is he or she committed and well established as an investment advisor?

Always Check Credentials Before Investing

Once you find someone you're interested in working with, especially if the investment advisor is independent, invest a bit of time to verify his or her credentials. One way to do this is to ask for client referrals and then contact those people to determine if they're happy with the services they've received. If the person is a Registered Investment Advisor with the Securities and Exchange Commission (SEC), you can request to see their Form ADV, which they're required to file annually. You can visit the SEC's Web page to checkout brokers and investment advisors, *www.sec.gov/investor/brokers.htm*.

According to the SEC,

"Federal or state securities laws require brokers, investment advisers, and their firms to be licensed or registered, and to make important information public. ... Before you invest or pay for any investment advice, make sure your brokers, investment advisers, and investment adviser representatives are licensed. ... The Central Registration Depository (or "CRD") is a computerized database that contains information about most brokers, their representatives, and the firms they work for. You can ask either your state securities regulator or the National Association of Securities Dealers to provide you with information from the CRD.

"People or firms that get paid to give advice about investing in securities generally must register with either the SEC or the state securities agency where they have their principal place of business. To find out about investment advisers and whether they are properly registered, read their registration forms, called the "Form ADV." The Form ADV has two parts. Part 1 has information about the adviser's business and whether they've had problems with regulators or clients. Part 2 outlines the adviser's services, fees, and strategies. Before you hire an investment adviser, always ask for and carefully read both parts of the ADV."

It's possible to view an advisor's most recent ADV form online, by visiting the Investment Adviser Public Disclosure Web site (*www.adviserinfo.sec.gov/IAPD/Content/IapdMain/iapd_SiteMap.aspx*).

If the investment advisor is a CFP or a CPA or has some other credential, you can contact the governing body for that credential to make sure he or she is a member in good standing or has not been the subject of any complaints. You can investigate a broker by contacting the National Association of Securities Dealers (800) 289-9999 (www.nasd.com). To do research about a CFP, you can visit the Certified Financial Planner Board of Standards' Web site at *www.cfp.com* or call the BrokerCheck Hotline at (888) 237-6275. The American Institute of Certified Public Accountants can be reached at (212) 596-6200 (*www.aicpa.org*).

Another way to determine if the investment advisor has been the subject of any complaints is to contact the local Better Business Bureau (*www.bbb.org*) in the area where he or she is based.

Warning

CHURNING: WATCH OUT Some of the most common complaints investors have related to their investment advisor are that he or she recommends unsuitable investments, the portfolio is not sufficiently diversified, the advisor misrepresents or omits important information, and he or she generates excessive or unnecessary activity within the account in order to increase commissions (a process called *churning*.)

An investment advisor might possess one or more accreditations, certifications, degrees, or licenses. Choose someone who has the knowledge, expertise and experience, and resources you want and need.

A CFP designation demonstrates that the person is highly proficient in many areas of personal finance and has undergone extensive training. A CPA (an accountant) may be beneficial in helping you deal with the tax implications of your investments. If someone claims to have a specific credential, determine what the credential means and how it will benefit you. Also, make sure you pay only for the expertise you actually need for choosing and/or managing your investments.

Understanding the Fees You'll Pay

When you hire an independent investment advisor, you'll need to pay for the advice and services offered. However, the method of compensation will vary.

Some investment advisors are paid a fee directly by their clients. This can be an hourly fee for advice. For ongoing portfolio management, annual compensation is often calculated based on a percentage of the total value of a client's portfolio (typically around one percent).

Some investment advisors represent the products and/or services of specific companies. For recommending or selling specific investments to clients, he or she receives a commission. Investment advisors can also be compensated through a combination of fees plus commissions.

Another alternative is that you receive investment advice and guidance from an expert who is employed by the mutual fund company with which you're investing, such as Fidelity Investments, T. Rowe Price, Charles Schwab, or Vanguard. These experts will offer you virtually the same services as independent investment advisors, but with one significant difference—the financial expert or advisor who is employed by the investment company is biased and loyal to that company. In other words, the financial advisor who helps you for free when you contact Fidelity Investments, for example, is never going to recommend a T. Rowe Price or Vanguard mutual fund.

By hiring an independent investment advisor and paying his or her fees, you'll hopefully receive personalized, expert, and unbiased advice and portfolio management services. This approach is typically more suited for someone with a portfolio worth over $50,000 or $100,000 and for investors whose portfolios include more than just mutual funds. For smaller investors, it is typically adequate to take advantage of the advice and portfolio management services offered by companies like Fidelity, T. Rowe Price, Charles Schwab, and Vanguard.

One big advantage to using the investment advisors employed by the mutual fund companies is that their fees are often built into what you'll already be paying to purchase and own the mutual fund(s). Because companies like Fidelity, T. Rowe Price, Charles Schwab, and Vanguard offer such a diverse range of mutual funds, the advice you receive may be company-specific, but it can still be extremely beneficial. Also, your overall portfolio can still be properly diversified.

When working with an investment advisor who is employed by a specific company and who is loyal to that company, you still want to ensure that the advisor is qualified to provide the type of personalized investment advice you need. Thus, ask about the person's credentials, experience, and area of expertise. Someone who is an expert in retirement planning might not be the best person to offer advice on investing for your child's education, for example.

The investment advisor (or retirement planning service representative) employed by the company with which you opt to invest should spend one-on-one time with you discussing your financial and investment goals, your comfort

Investing Tip

WATCH THE FEES You always want to ask about the fees you'll be paying for the advice, portfolio management, and other services you receive. These fees may be in addition to the fees you'll be paying to buy, hold, and redeem mutual fund shares. Determine what the fees are, how they're calculated, what you'll ultimately be paying, and when the fees will be charged.

level with risk, and your current financial situation, just as an independent investment advisor would. He or she should then guide you to select the right combination of mutual funds managed by that company, based on your objectives and time horizon.

Advice from an Expert: Stuart Ritter, CFP

Stuart Ritter is a Certified Financial Planner employed by T. Rowe Price's Financial Planning Services Group. In this interview, he offers advice to first-time and inexperienced mutual fund investors and explains some of the services you can expect to receive when you invest with a well-respected mutual fund company, such as T. Rowe Price.

Ritter graduated from college with a degree in electrical engineering, but returned to school to obtain a master's degree in political science. Ultimately, he started working in the benefits field and in different aspects of financial planning. Nine years ago, he was hired by T. Rowe Price and simultaneously earned his CFP designation. Through his position with T. Rowe Price's Financial Planning Services Group, Ritter

Investing Tip

To learn more about the services and mutual funds offered by T. Rowe Price, call (800) 225-5132 or visit *www.troweprice.com*.

spends much of his time offering investment advice to clients and helping them to achieve their financial goals. He also teaches personal financial planning at several community colleges in the Maryland area where he is based.

What services does T. Rowe Price offer to its mutual funds investors?

Stuart Ritter: "T. Rowe Price is a firm that offers investment management for individuals and institutions worldwide. We help people better reach their financial goals through our investment management expertise. We provide experience in selecting individual investments within the context of our clients' investing strategy. Mutual funds are the main investment tool we use to achieve this. We offer a simple, convenient and effective way for people to do their investing. We also help people develop their investing strategies.

"If someone comes to us and says they want to be able to put their child through college in 15 years, we help them develop the investment strategies that will allow them to do that. We'll help them set their goals, develop, and then manage their portfolio. We focus not just on our mutual fund products, but on the process for achieving someone's financial goals. T. Rowe Price puts a lot of effort into educating people and walking them through the decision-making process.

"One analogy I use is comparing investing to graduating from college. A college student can randomly pick a bunch of classes, but if he or she wants to graduate within a certain time period and earn some sort of degree, they're required to focus on a major and complete specific classes in a predefined sequence. Those classes must meet the requirements of the major, as well as the graduation requirements of the college or university. To help students plan their course schedules, they can tap the expertise of advisors and teachers.

"T. Rowe Price offers the same philosophy when it comes to investing in mutual funds. We help people choose the right investments that will allow them to achieve their goals. We walk people through the decision-making processes to choose the right combination of mutual funds, plus provide a wide selection of mutual funds for them to invest in."

If someone is interested in investing in mutual funds and calls on a company like T. Rowe Price, what is the process the investor will go through to get started?

Stuart Ritter: "The first thing we spend time doing is developing an understanding of each customer and what they're trying to accomplish. Some people come to us, know exactly what they want, and simply want us to execute their wishes as quickly and efficiently as possible. Other people call up and want a lot of help and advice. For these people, we'll walk them through the decision-making process. We figure out what they want from a financial standpoint. Our approach is consistent with all of our customers, but the solutions we provide are specific to each customer."

In your option, what is it about mutual funds that makes them so attractive to investors?

Stuart Ritter: "They're a convenient way for people to achieve their financial goals through investing. When you invest in mutual funds, you receive instant diversification, you can get started with relatively little money, plus your investments are professionally managed. These are all things that are difficult to achieve on your own, but easy to achieve with mutual funds. When people are looking to invest, mutual funds offer a simple approach, which can save time."

What are some of the drawbacks to mutual funds?

Stuart Ritter: "There are costs associated with mutual funds. It's important to pay attention to these costs. I recommend asking directly about the fees. Offer a dollar amount that you'll be investing, and ask specifically what the fees will be for that size investment. Also, take the investment itself out of the picture. Ask how much you'd pay in fees if you invested, say, $1,000 into a mutual fund that earns nothing for a year. What would the fees be? If the fee is one per-cent and you invest $1,000, you'll know you'll be paying $10 in fees and expenses. Also, ask if there are any other fees, such as sales charges, transaction fees, redemption fees, or fees you'll be charged in other circumstances. Ask how the person you're talking to is compensated and whether the investment decisions you make have any impact on how much they're paid."

If someone opts to utilize the services and investment opportunities offered by T. Rowe Price, does he or she still need to hire an independent investment advisor?

Stuart Ritter: "Generally not. We provide guidance to peo-ple all the time, which is one of our areas of expertise. We understand the questions that need to be asked, diagnose the problem, and we know how to map out a solution. Based on an investor's goals and needs, we can help them establish a well-rounded and diversified portfolio. We also understand the tax benefits associated with investing in cer-tain types of funds in order to achieve specific goals."

An important investing concern is diversification. If some-one invests only in various T. Rowe Price mutual funds, for example, is that considered diversification or should the money be spread into funds managed by other compa-nies as well?

Stuart Ritter: "Diversification means not putting too much of your money into any one sector of the market or into any one individual stock. If you put together your mutual fund portfolio correctly, you can use all funds managed by one company, because the holdings of those funds will be adequately diversified.

"One of the things we do to make the diversification process even simpler is offer specific mutual funds that invest in groups of mutual funds. So, instead of purchasing three, four, or five different types of mutual funds from T. Rowe Price, for example, you can invest in one fund that then invests in many different mutual funds. This means you can establish a complete and diversified portfolio by investing in a single fund.

"This approach is particularly useful for retirement planning or lifecycle investing. We have 'retirement date funds,' which are specifically designed for retirement planning. You pick the fund that is closest to your retirement date. This fund will then manage the mix of stock, bond, and short-term investment funds appropriate to the time horizon. As you get older, the fund's holdings automatically shift from stock to bond funds. This is the easiest retirement planning solution we offer, plus the investor benefits from our fund's professional management.

"The T. Rowe Price 'Spectrum Funds' are similar types of funds that invest in other mutual funds, but they can be used for other investment purposes besides retirement. The difference is that these funds don't automatically shift from stock to bond funds over time. Mutual funds that invest in other mutual funds are called '*funds of funds.*'"

FUND OF FUNDS A mutual fund that invests in other mutual funds. A fund of funds makes it easier for an investor to benefit from maximum diversification to achieve specific financial goals by investing into only one  **Mutual Fund Key Term** fund and reaping the benefits of several or many funds. Instead of paying fees for several funds, the fees tend to be a bit higher for a fund of funds because the investor is paying management fees twice.

LIFE-CYCLE FUND A mutual fund in which the holdings change as time passes, using a systematic plan for adjusting asset allocation according to the target of the fund. Also known as *target-date fund* or *target-maturity fund*. For retirement investing, age-based life-cycle investing allows an investor to choose a fund based on a target date for retirement. As with any mutual fund, the mix of holdings will vary from fund to fund even if the funds have the same objective. For example, 20 years from the target date, one retirement 2025 fund is invested 67 percent in stocks, 28 percent in bonds, and 5 percent in a money market while another retirement 2025 fund holds 59 percent stocks and 41 percent bonds.

For someone who is starting to invest, is it OK to create an initial portfolio composed only of mutual funds?

Stuart Ritter: "Yes. That's fine if you are first starting out, unless you're starting off with a large amount of money,

Investing Tip

ABOUT T. ROWE PRICE The T. Rowe Price Spectrum Funds include the Spectrum Growth Fund, Spectrum Income Fund, and Spectrum International Fund. These are three broadly diversified funds of funds that invest in other T. Rowe Price funds. The fund of funds retirement funds from T. Rowe Price include the Retirement 2010 Fund, Retirement 2015 Fund, Retirement 2020 Fund, Retirement 2025 Fund, Retirement 2030 Fund, Retirement 2035 Fund, and so on. You can download a prospectus for any of these funds from the T. Rowe Price Web site (*www.troweprice.com*).

Fidelity Investment, for example, also offers a similar set of funds suitable for retirement planning, called Fidelity Freedom Funds. For more information, visit *www.fidelity.com* or call (800) 343-3548. Vanguard also offers life-style funds—its LifeStrategy funds and its Target Retirement funds. For more information, visit *www.vanguard.com* or call (877) 662-7447.

---

such as $50,000 or $100,000. With a relatively small amount of money, you can obtain the necessary diversification using mutual funds. For beginners, I often recommend investing in a fund of funds."

In addition to investment advice, what other resources should an investor expect from a mutual fund company?

Stuart Ritter: "The T. Rowe Price Web site, for example, is loaded with a wide range of tools and resources, including articles and introductory information about investing and mutual funds. We also offer analytical, research, and online-based portfolio management tools, many of which are available free of charge. If you're interested in making your own investment decisions or managing your own portfolio, working with a company that offers a wide range of online tools and resources will be beneficial."

When an investor contacts a company like T. Rowe Price or Fidelity Investments for the first time, how can he or she determine if the representative is knowledgeable and experienced?

Stuart Ritter: "Ask questions. Most of the larger companies have a structure in place so anyone who works with clients can utilize the vast resources of the company, even if they themselves are not a CFP, for example. Whomever you work with should be able to easily draw on the expertise within their company using very structured methods. An analogy is that in the medical field, you don't always need to talk to a surgeon. In many cases, a nurse or doctor can answer your medical questions and address your health needs.

"I recommend asking the people you're working with not just about the credentials they possess, but what they had to do in order to earn their credentials. Also, ask what tools and resources are available to them to help you, the investor, make intelligent decisions."

How much time should someone plan on investing to establish and then manage a mutual fund portfolio?

Stuart Ritter: "The answer to this question depends on the approach the person wants to take. If you're going to be choosing your own mutual funds and the other contents of your portfolio yourself, you could invest several hours per week for the rest of your life managing your portfolio. If you'll be investing solely in mutual funds, you're probably talking about a time commitment of several hours every three to six months or so, to review your portfolio. In some situations, once your mutual fund portfolio is set up, you'll only need to check on it once or twice per year, which requires a very minimal time commitment.

"You'll probably need to invest some time upfront to establish your portfolio and to discuss your needs with the investment advisor you work with. If you have other investments beyond mutual funds, it will require more time to manage them."

What does a periodic review of a mutual fund portfolio entail?

Stuart Ritter: "Always focus on your financial goal and your time horizon. Ask yourself, for your goal and time horizon, what should be in your target portfolio? How much should you have invested in stock and bond funds? Next, compare your target with what your portfolio currently contains and determine if adjustments need to be made.

"When you review your portfolio every three to six months, you should not worry about what the hottest trends are at that time and then shift all of your money there. Your time horizon should be your primary driver for the strategy you put together. If your time horizon is 30 years until retirement, what happens in any given three-month period is not that important. It's essential to keep things in perspective. Regularly reviewing your portfolio does not mean you should shift everything around on a regular basis."

When someone is evaluating a mutual fund, what are some of the specific things to evaluate?

Stuart Ritter: "First, determine how that fund will fit into your portfolio. A fund can't really be evaluated on its own. For example, if you have a medical problem, you can't just ask, 'Is tetracycline a good drug to take?' After all, it would depend on what's wrong with you. For mutual funds, you need to understand how it will fit into your portfolio and then determine if it's a good investment for you. Once you know you want your portfolio to have a specific mix of stocks or bonds, for example, and you know your timeline, you can choose funds that will help you achieve those investing objectives.

"After determining the type of fund you want to add to your portfolio, then you can look at each individual fund's expenses and fees, its holdings, the fund manager's experience, and its long-term performance. Every mutual fund you add to your portfolio should have a specific role you want it to play in order to achieve your financial objectives.

"You can also compare a fund's performance, risk, fees, fund manager's tenure, and other information with other similar funds in the same category. Or, you can compare a fund's performance against a benchmark, such as the S&P 500 index."

There are a lot of analytical and research tools available to help investors evaluate mutual funds. Is it necessary for a novice to use some or all of these tools?

Stuart Ritter: "How much you want to understand about your investments is a personal decision. Most of us use power steering when we're driving our cars, but few people really know or care how power steering works. Keep the information you have about your investments in perspective. There is a lot of information out there. It's important to focus only on the information you'll need to achieve your financial goals. Don't get overwhelmed or bogged down with information overload.

"There is no magic statistic, or a number you should look for when choosing the perfect fund. It's all about finding the right combination of investments to achieve your goals. The biggest misconception people have about mutual funds is that they're way more complicated than they actually are. People think investing is hard, complicated, and very time-consuming. This does not have to be the case."

What is one of the biggest mistakes people make with their mutual fund investments?

Stuart Ritter: "People misunderstand the risks of investing. People's perspectives when they're thinking about risk are often not in line with their time horizon. For example, if someone has a 30-year time horizon, they'll overemphasize what happens over a three-month period. Measuring what happens over a period of several months, when you're looking at an investment time of decades, is insignificant."

How concerned should an investor be with the level of risk?

Stuart Ritter: "Everything is about balance and trade-offs. When people think about risk, they're worried that the value of their investment might go down. The question to ask, however, is the impact that risk will have over a prede-termined time period. A drop in an investment's value for a few months right now is insignificant if you won't need that money for ten or 20 years. The level of risk associated with an investment must be put into the appropriate context.

"People invest because at some point they want to buy something. It may be a new home, college tuition, a trip around the world, or a comfortable retirement. What people need to consider is the cost of what they want to buy, but take into account inflation. So, they need to consider what the cost will be of what they want to purchase in the future. When someone says they don't want to take on risk, they may choose to avoid the stock market. This allows them to eliminate some risk, but they may now be taking on risk associated with a reduction in their money's purchasing power because of inflation. If they leave their money in a savings account for 20 years, the interest they'll earn won't keep up with inflation. This means they'll need to save significantly more to wind up with the amount of money they'll eventually need.

"The trade-off is short-term market volatility versus purchasing power. If people avoid one, they'll take on a lot more of the other. The key is to balance the two for the time horizon you're investing for. For the long term, purchasing power is more of a concern. For the short term, purchasing power isn't that big of a deal, but stock volatility, for example, should be a concern."

Do you have any other mutual fund investing advice?

Stuart Ritter: "People are always waiting for the right time to invest. The right time is now. If the market is down, people often opt to wait until it goes up, which is actually counterproductive. People need to get started as soon as they know what their goal is and they can gather the money to invest. For most people, mutual funds should form the core of their investment portfolio.

"I also recommend putting your investment strategy on autopilot by setting up an automatic investment plan, so money is deducted from your paycheck or checking account and automatically invested on a regular basis."

What's Next

Now you have a basic understanding of the pros and cons of mutual funds, you've set some investment goals and a time horizon for achieving those goals, and you understand how to find a competent investment advisor. The next chapter delves into the many types of mutual funds, including stock and bond funds. You'll learn when investing in specific types of mutual funds is appropriate, how to diversify your portfolio of funds, and how to determine if a specific fund fits within your portfolio based on your goals and time horizon.

The Anatomy of a Mutual Fund

WHAT'S IN THIS CHAPTER

- Learn about the various types of mutual funds
- Understand a fund's prospectus
- Six things you should know about a fund before investing
- The fees associated with mutual funds
- The 411 on exchange-traded funds (ETFs)
- An interview with a mutual fund manager

I n Chapter 1, you learned the basics of mutual funds and how investors can use them to achieve specific financial goals. As you've probably guessed, there's a lot more still to learn about mutual funds before you should consider investing in them.

This chapter will help you better understand mutual funds and how various types of funds can be used to achieve specific objectives. The first step, however, is to carefully review your financial goals, calculate how much you have to invest, and determine the time horizon for your investments. With this information, you can more easily put together your investment portfolio by choosing specific types of mutual funds that will fit well within that portfolio.

Portfolio asset allocation refers to the combination of types of mutual funds and other investments in your portfolio. As you'll discover, someone with a conservative investment strategy will have a very different combination of investments than someone adopting a more aggressive and riskier investment strategy.

Mutual funds typically fall into one of three main types based primarily on their objective—*growth, income,* or *growth and income.* Mutual funds are also categorized based on their primary holdings. The holdings of a fund determine its risk level and potential for performance. While the holdings of a mutual fund are diversified, that diversification is limited to the focus of that particular fund. For example, a blue-chip growth fund will have at least 80 percent of its holdings in blue-chip stocks. To truly have a diversified portfolio, you'll probably want to invest in a handful of mutual funds with vastly different investment strategies or use a fund of funds.

BLUE-CHIP STOCK A generic term for the stocks of large companies (worth more than $3 billion) with a history of profitability, stability, and above-average performance. **Mutual Fund Key Term** The name comes from poker, where the high-value chips are traditionally blue.

Since you'll be entrusting your money to fund managers, this chapter concludes with an interview with Larry J. Puglia, the fund manager for T. Rowe Price's Blue Chip Growth Fund. From this interview, you'll learn more about what a successful fund manager does and how he or she does it.

Investing Tip

THE MUTUAL FUND ANALYST Morningstar (*www.morningstar.com*), which is perhaps the world's most respected mutual fund analyst firm, uses a style box (a nine-box grid) to quickly categorize funds based on asset allocation and primary investment strategy. You'll learn more about the resources Morningstar offers to investors within Chapter 5. These resources can help you select the right funds to add to your portfolio, based on your financial goals and time horizon.

Types of Mutual Funds by Strategy

Knowing that virtually every mutual fund follows an investment strategy that's intended for growth (increase in value over time), for income (dividends and capital gains distribu-tions), or for both growth and income, you should decide what type of overall investment strategy is most appropriate for your goals and time horizon, before choosing specific funds.

Life-cycle funds (introduced in the previous chapter) are a hybrid in that their investment strategy changes over time. For example, if you invest in a life-cycle fund for retirement, that fund will be more aggressive early on and include more stock funds, international, and global funds in its holdings, and then, as you get older and closer to needing your money, the fund will shift into less risky investments, such as bond funds. The change in investment strategy and asset allocation of the fund is automatically controlled by the fund manager. As a result, you do not need to drastically alter your portfolio over time. The required changes in asset allocation and invest-ment strategy are made by the fund manager.

Categories of Mutual Funds by Their Primary Holdings

After determining the investment strategy you'd like for each mutual fund in your portfolio, the next step is to choose indi-vidual funds from specific categories that will help you meet your financial goals. These are the most popular categories of mutual funds.

Stock Funds

Stock funds are mutual funds that are at least 80 percent

invested in stocks. A stock represents ownership in a publicly traded company. Different stock mutual funds invest in different types of stocks. These differences determine the level of risk in the funds, in terms of how they perform and how investors feel about them.

Some stock mutual funds invest according to the size of companies. There are funds that invest primarily in *large-cap stocks* or blue chip stocks, such as IBM or General Electric. Investing in stocks of large companies that have long been profitable and stable carries a risk that is relatively low. Some funds focus on investing in *mid-cap stocks* (companies of moderate market value) or *small-cap stocks* (smaller, less-established, and riskier companies).

Mutual Fund Key Term

MARKET CAPITALIZATION Total market value of a company, calculated as the number of shares outstanding multiplied by the current price of one share of the stock as quoted on a stock exchange. Capitalization is a common and convenient measure of the size of a company. In the U.S., there are generally three divisions of market capitalization, with varying dollar limits: large-cap (usually above $3 billion or $5 billion), mid-cap (usually between $500 million or $1 billion and $3 billion or $5 billion), and small-cap (usually below $500 million or $1 billion).

SMALL-CAP STOCK Company with a market capitalization below $500 million or $1 billion. These are typically smaller, less established companies, which means investment is riskier.

MID-CAP STOCK Company with a market capitalization between $500 million and $1 billion or $3 billion or $5 billion. These are typically more growth-oriented companies and are less risky than small-cap stocks but riskier than large-cap stocks.

LARGE-CAP STOCK Company with a market capitalization above $3 billion or $5 billion. These are well-established companies, like General Electric or IBM, which grow more slowly but are very stable.

Stock-based funds might invest only in domestic companies, while others focus on international companies. *Global* funds use a mix of stock investments from domestic and international companies. *Emerging markets* funds invest in small, developing countries and in companies within those countries.

Country-specific funds invest primarily in specific countries and in stocks issued by companies located within those countries. For example, Fidelity Investments offers Canada Fund, China Region Fund, Europe Fund, Japan Fund, Nordic Fund, and Pacific Basin Fund.

Sector funds focus on investing in companies within a specific sector or industry, such as health care or technology or energy. *Index* funds are designed to mimic the performance of a certain index, such as the *S&P 500* or the *Dow Jones Industrial Average* (DJIA).

Stock funds tend to be the most volatile mutual funds and carry the most risk. Of course, the types of stocks in a fund portfolio greatly determines its risk level. For example, a fund

Mutual Fund Key Term

INDEX A hypothetical portfolio of securities intended to be representative of a particular market or sector of a market, to be used as a measure of changes in that market or sector and as a benchmark for measuring performance. The Dow Jones Industrial Average and the Standard & Poor's 500 are two of the best-known indexes and the benchmarks most commonly used for the U.S. stock market.

DOW JONES INDUSTRIAL AVERAGE (DJIA) A stock market index that consists of 30 of the largest and most widely held public companies in the United States. It is used as a measure of how the stock market overall is performing. There are a variety of mutual funds designed to mimic the performance of this index.

S&P 500 A stock market index consisting of the stocks of 500 large corporations that trade on the major U.S. stock exchanges and are considered leaders in leading industries. The S&P 500 is an important index of large-cap U.S. stocks, second only to the Dow Jones Industrial Index. Many index funds track the performance of the S&P 500.

INDEX FUND A mutual fund intended to replicate the performance of the market or a sector by maintaining a portfolio of holdings that mirror the composition of a market or sector index. The most common index fund is based on the S&P 500, with holdings of all 500 stocks in the same percentages as the index. Other indexes that mutual funds emulate include the Russell 2000, the Wilshire 5000, and the NASDAQ 100. Index funds outperform most other mutual funds, in part because they are managed passively so their expenses are lower and in part because most managed mutual funds fail to perform better than broad indexes such as the S&P 500.

invested in blue chips will be much less risky than a fund invested in companies in international and emerging markets.

Bond Funds (Fixed-Income Securities)

A bond fund invests mainly in bonds in order to generate high income and/or preserve capital while taking on minimal risk. The performance of these funds will vary, based on the types of bonds they hold (short-term, intermediate-term, or long-term). Some bond funds are tax-free or offer special tax benefits to certain types of investors. One benefit to bond funds is that they can be used to generate an ongoing monthly income for the investor, which is why they're also called *fixed-income securities*.

A *bond* is a loan. Corporations or governments (local, state, and federal) can issue bonds. They're a promise to pay back the amount of money borrowed, plus interest, within a predetermined period of time (their *maturity*). Bonds are considered a less risky investment than stocks, but they are not without risk.

MATURITY Length of time until the principal amount of a bond is to be repaid in full. This may be expressed in units of time or as a maturity date.

Mutual Fund Key Term

The bond market as a whole behaves differently than the stock market. Bonds and stocks often move in opposite directions. As a result, many investors use bond funds to balance their portfolios and to diversify their investments. Bond funds tend to be used by people looking to generate a regular income from their investments. For example, someone close to retirement will most likely invest in bond funds to reduce investment risk and generate a monthly income.

Just as there are different types of stock funds, there are also different types of bond funds. They are typically categorized in these four groups:

- Corporate bond funds—funds that invest primarily in bonds issued by U.S.-based corporations
- Mortgage-backed securities funds—funds that are composed mainly of residential mortgages
- Municipal bond funds—funds that invest primarily in tax-exempt bonds that are issued by state and local governments
- U.S. government bond funds—funds invested in bonds issued by the United States Treasury and in other securities issued by the federal government

Bond funds can also be categorized by their maturity date. A bond fund that invests in short-term bonds means that the holdings have no more than two years before their maturity. Many short-term bond funds generate better returns than money market funds. Intermediate-term bond funds tend to invest in holdings that mature within two to ten years. A long-term bond fund typically invests in holdings with a maturity date exceeding ten years.

Investing in individual bonds can be a complex process. Investing in bond funds, however, is easy. Then, investors can rely on the fund managers to handle all of the complex decisions involved with investing in bonds.

Money Market Funds

Money market funds are referred to as a *cash equivalent*, because they're virtually as liquid as cash. However, they're a little riskier for investors than a standard bank savings account, which has absolutely no risk associated with it—other than inflation risk, the risk that the purchasing power of the savings will decrease due to a rise in prices. Money market funds invest in short-term instruments, such as U.S. Treasury bills, commercial paper (unsecured, short-term debt instruments issued by corporations), certificates of deposit, and repurchase agreements. Money market funds are ideal short-term investments (less than one to two years) and can be used to balance a portfolio's diversification.

Money invested in money markets can be withdrawn quickly and with no penalties, which often makes them a more attractive investment option than *certificates of deposit* (CDs), which lock up the money invested for a specified length of time, or bonds, which have maturity dates.

Money market funds are *not* insured by the FDIC, but there's very little risk with them because the money is held in very safe investments, such as Treasury bills. When investing in a money market fund, you can typically expect a return on your investment of about four to six percent per year, which is similar to what you'd earn investing in CDs. This return is significantly lower than what investments in most stock or bond funds could generate over the long term, but money market funds are intended to be safe, short-term investments.

The larger mutual fund companies, such as Fidelity, T. Rowe Price, and Vanguard, all offer a wide range of money market funds, some of which are tax-free.

Index Funds

Index funds are a type of stock fund, but with a very specific investment strategy. The goal of an index fund is to mimic the performance of one particular stock market index, such as the Standard & Poor's 500 (S&P 500) Index.

The S&P 500 Index, created in 1976, is considered a benchmark for overall stock market performance. The index consists of the 500 most widely held companies based on common stock, from a wide range of industries. It's weighted by market capitalization. (In other words, the companies are not represented equally but rather in proportion to the market value of each company.) This index includes General Electric, Microsoft, Exxon Mobil, Pfizer, Citigroup, Wal-Mart, Intel, IBM, and other such industry leaders. Over time, the S&P 500 has been proven to outperform many popular mutual funds.

Virtually all of the popular mutual fund companies offer at least one *no-load* index fund based on the S&P 500. For example, there's the Dreyfus S&P 500 Index, Fidelity Spartan 500 Index, Schwab S&P 500 Fund, Vanguard 500 Index Fund, and the T. Rowe Price Equity Index 500. Out of all the index funds out there, the Vanguard 500 Index Fund, with over $89.4 billion in assets, is the most popular among investors. It was also the first index fund ever created to mimic the S&P 500, in 1976.

For an investor, index funds offer three advantages over other types of mutual funds: they often have a much lower expense ratio, they tend to perform better, and they're less risky. In addition to investing in index mutual funds, you can also invest in the indexes themselves. Well, not exactly, since an index is a statistical calculation. But you can invest in *exchange-traded funds*, which we'll discuss later in this chapter.

Investing Tip

MOTLEY FOOL You can find a list of index funds from many companies and compare how they're performing by visiting The Motley Fool Web site (*www.fool.com/mutualfunds/indexfunds/table01.htm*).

Industry or Sector Funds

An industry or sector fund is a mutual fund that invests in a specific industry or a sector of the economy, such as air transportation, automotive, banking, biotechnology, brokerage and investment management, chemicals, computers, construction and housing, consumer industries, defense and aerospace, electronics, energy, financial services, health care, insurance, multimedia, natural gas, pharmaceuticals, real estate, retailing, technology, telecommunications, and transportation.

Investors interested in this type of focused investment can finds funds for virtually every industry. Because of their narrower focus, these funds tend to be riskier than funds that are diversified among many industries.

Industry or sector funds perform well when the demand for products or services from that industry or sector is strong. When demand falls, so does the performance of these funds. This makes them much more volatile than other types of mutual funds. Such funds in a portfolio require more attention and monitoring from the investor.

Specialty Funds

These are funds with a special purpose. A specialty fund might invest only in companies that adhere to specific environmental, social, moral, or religious beliefs. For example, there are "environmentally conscious" funds that invest only in companies that help to preserve the well-being of the planet. There are specialty funds that focus on community investment or invest only in companies that exhibit responsible human rights employment policies. Other specialty mutual funds affiliate with a specific charitable organization or cause. For example, American Century Investments (888 340-4545/*www.livestrong-portfolios.com*) offers its LiveStrong Portfolios, a series of mutual funds that support the mission of the Lance Armstrong Foundation, which is to inspire and empower people and families affected by cancer.

People who invest in socially responsible mutual funds and other investments are called *social investors*. To learn more about social investing, there are a variety of resources, including the following:

- **Domini Social Investments**—(800) 762-6814, *www.domini.com*
- **goodfunds.com**—(206) 782-1205, (800) 940-1747, *www.goodfunds.com*
- **Principles for Responsible Investing**—*www.unpri.org*
- **SocialFunds.com**—(802) 251-0500, *www.socialfunds.com*
- **Social Investment Forum**—(202) 872-5319, *www.socialinvest.org*
- **The GreenMoney Journal**—(800) 849-8751, *www.greenmoneyjournal.com*

Warning

WATCH THE SOCIAL FEES Unfortunately, many socially responsible mutual funds have higher fees than other mutual funds. So, before investing, first make sure the fund actually adheres to the socially responsible investment practices it promotes. Second, ensure that the fees aren't so high that adding the fund to your portfolio would not be financially practical.

The flip side to socially responsible investing is—you guessed it—"socially irresponsible investing." This implies that greedy investors go out of their way to invest in companies or pursue investment opportunities that can potentially be harmful to other people, the environment, or the planet. There are mutual funds, for example, that focus on investing in highly profitable tobacco companies, alcoholic beverage companies, casinos, and companies that have shown little or no concern for the environment, that use overseas child labor, or that test their products on animals. These funds can, of course, earn investors money, but you have to decide whether or not being socially responsible is important.

Funds of Funds

Funds of funds, as discussed in Chapter 3, are mutual funds that invest in other mutual funds in order to create the ultimate in diversified portfolios. For many novice investors, a fund of funds is a fast, simple, and easy way to invest without taking on too much risk or needing to spend a significant amount of time creating a portfolio.

Fund Type: Risks and Returns

By now, you should understand that the type of mutual fund you choose will impact the level of risk you assume for that investment and the return you can expect. The following is a brief summary of the performance you can expect from certain types of mutual funds. This information will help you fit appropriate types of funds into your portfolio.

Diversified bond funds. For investors looking for a significant level of income, these funds tend to invest in high- and medium-grade, non-money market securities, such as corporate bonds and notes, government securities, and securities that are backed by mortgages.

Emerging markets funds. International mutual funds that invest in emerging or developing countries are typically used by investors looking for capital growth. These funds can be significantly riskier than international funds that invest in First-World countries.

Equity growth funds. These mutual funds are ideal if you're looking for long-term growth, but not necessarily interested in dividend payments.

Growth funds. These mutual funds are best suited to investors looking to achieve growth over a long term. Growth funds typically invest in U.S.-based companies, so they're less risky than funds with international holdings.

High-yield bond funds. For investors looking for a significant income, these funds typically invest in a wide selection of high-yield corporate bonds, as well as other securities.

International bond funds. By investing in high-quality bonds issued overseas, these funds seek to generate high income.

International growth funds. These funds are good for investors looking for long-term growth and willing to take on extra risk in hopes of higher returns.

Large-company value funds. These funds typically focus on the largest U.S.-based companies. They're intended as long-term investments where income is less important than growth.

Small-company funds. These funds are suitable for investors with long-term time horizons. The holdings of these funds tend to be smaller, more volatile, U.S.-based companies.

Why Portfolio Asset Allocation Is Important

Different types of mutual funds perform differently and generate vastly different returns over time, based on their holdings and the investment strategies employed by the fund managers. So, depending on your own investment strategy and goals, you'll want to diversify your portfolio in a way that minimizes your risk, maximizes returns, and enables you to achieve your financial objectives within your time horizon. This means coming up with a comfortable balance of stock funds and bond funds and combining funds with a strictly domestic focus and funds with a sometimes riskier international focus. You could also opt to diversify with global funds, mixing domestic and international.

The process of mixing and matching types of funds and investments is called *portfolio asset allocation*. Over the time you own your portfolio, your focus or goals may change, in which case, you will need to adjust your asset allocation accordingly. If you're starting to invest right now for your

Investing Tip

INTELLIGENT ALLOCATION When setting your portfolio's asset allocation, think in terms of when you'll need access to your money and how long you'll need the money to last. If you're planning to retire in 30 years, you have that much time to generate the best growth and highest return on your investment possible. Then, you'll need to use that money over a time that's indefinite. If you're planning to buy a home in five years, you have that much time and then you'll need all of your money at once.

Investing Tip

HELP ONLINE Many of the mutual fund companies offer online tools to help investors achieve the appropriate portfolio asset allocation. For example, you'll find an Investment Strategy Planner that is free of charge on the T. Rowe Price Web site, at *www.troweprice.com/investmenttools*.

retirement, but you won't need the money for 30 or more years, your investment strategy and asset allocation for the next several years will be vastly different from your strategy and asset allocation 20 or 25 years from now as you approach retirement age.

Of course, everyone's situation is different, so it's important to create a portfolio that you're comfortable with and that will generate the returns you want in terms of your particular goals. The mutual fund company you opt to work with will help you determine appropriate portfolio asset allocation and balance. The following are some samples of asset allocation formulas that you can apply according to your time horizon and goals.

Short Term

If you have money to invest for only a short term (less than two years), you'll probably want to take on little risk to protect your principle, but generate the best return possible. Consequently, highly liquid, short-term investments (money market funds, CDs, etc.) are the most suitable.

Recommended Asset Allocation Formula

Short-Term Investments:	100%
Bonds:	0%
Stocks:	0%
International:	0%

Conservative

Regardless of your time horizon, if you want to develop a well-rounded and diversified portfolio that will provide respectable returns and keep your risk low, you should take a conservative approach. The following is a sample asset allocation for a conservative investor—someone who prefers to play it safe, but who wants a better return on investment than is possible from a savings account, a CD, or a money market fund.

Recommended Asset Allocation Formula

Short-Term Investments:	30%
Bonds:	50%
Stocks:	20%
International:	0%

Balanced

For the average investor who is willing to take on some risk and who is looking for a good return on investment, a balanced investment strategy for asset allocation is appropriate. As you can see, 45 percent of the portfolio is invested in stock funds, which are more volatile than bond funds or short-term investments. A small portion of the portfolio can also be invested in international funds, which tend to be riskier, but have the potential for high returns. The riskier investments are balanced or offset by the less risky or less volatile investments in a balanced asset allocation strategy.

Recommended Asset Allocation Formula

Short-Term Investments:	10%
Bonds:	40%
Stocks:	45%
International:	5%

Growth

Someone who is working with a long time horizon (ten years or more) can focus on growth, generating the best returns possible for building wealth. To achieve this, the portfolio's asset allocation should focus on stocks (or stock funds), but be rounded out with other types of investments.

Recommended Asset Allocation Formula

Short-Term Investments:	5%
Bonds:	25%
Stocks:	60%
International:	10%

Aggressive Growth

An investor who is working with a time horizon of at least five years and who wants to see his or her portfolio grow dramatically will need to take on riskier investments, with a greater focus on stock funds and international investments.

This approach is definitely not suitable for everyone, especially investors who are uncomfortable with risk or who can't afford to lose too much money.

Recommended Asset Allocation Formula

Short-Term Investments:	0%
Bonds:	15%
Stocks:	70%
International:	15%

Extremely Aggressive

Imagine taking an aggressive investment strategy and putting it on steroids. That's an "extremely aggressive" strategy. The potential return is great, but the risks are significant. This type of investment strategy is more suitable for experienced investors who are not relying on the money they're investing to cover their living expenses and who hope to significantly build their cash reserves or wealth.

Recommended Asset Allocation Formula

Short-Term Investments:	0%
Bonds:	0%
Stocks:	80% or 90%
International:	20% or 10%

Always Read the Prospectus

Before investing in any mutual fund, be sure to read the prospectus. As discussed in Chapter 1, this is a document that outlines the details of the investment: it describes the fund's objectives, primary investment strategy, risks, expenses, past performance, and information about the fund's manager(s). The prospectus also explains exactly how to invest in the fund and how to redeem (sell) shares.

The prospectus for a mutual fund is available directly from the mutual fund company or from a broker for that fund. It can be obtained in person or by mail or downloaded from the company's Web site. There is no charge for the prospectus, which can be anywhere from 20 to 50 or more pages long.

As you read a prospectus, you'll often discover that it makes a strong sales pitch for the fund (since this document is intended to attract new investors), but that it also contains important facts, figures, and information about the fund you should know as an investor.

Investing Tip

READ THE PROSPECTUS Before investing in any mutual fund, take the time to read the prospectus. This will help you determine if the fund would be a suitable addition to your portfolio. For additional information about a specific fund, you can also use the research tools described in Chapter 5. For example, you can research a fund's Morningstar Star Rating or determine how a fund has performed in comparison with similar types of funds.

Anatomy of a Prospectus

There are thousands of mutual funds and each has a prospectus. Every prospectus follows the same basic format and structure, follows specific legal guidelines in terms of content, and conveys important information about the fund to potential investors. The following is a summary of the sections you'll find in virtually any mutual fund prospectus.

Investment Objective. In just a few sentences, the first page of a prospectus describes the fund's objective. Knowing this objective will help you determine if the fund will fit into your portfolio, based on your financial goals, your time horizon, and the asset allocation you're trying to achieve. Here are two examples. For the T. Row Price Blue Chip Growth Fund, the prospectus states, "The fund seeks to provide long-term capital growth. Income is a secondary objective." For Fidelity's Growth & Income Portfolio fund, the prospectus states, "Growth & Income Portfolio seeks high total return through a combination of current income and capital appreciation."

Investment Strategy. This section of a prospectus, also in the first few pages, describes in some detail the fund's investment strategy. Here, you may find several pages of text or a list of bulleted points outlining primary investment strategies and objectives.

Risks. This section of the prospectus will describe the level and types of risks the investor assumes when buying into the fund. For example, the prospectus for Fidelity's Growth & Income Portfolio fund lists "stock market volatility," "interest rate changes," "foreign exposure," and "issuer-specific changes" as the primary risks associated with the fund.

Past Performance. Here you'll find information about how the fund has performed. Again, past performance is *not* an indicator of future performance. However, knowing this information can help an investor determine how stable and well-managed a particular fund is and provide some insight into future potential returns. A prospectus will typically describe year-by-year returns and average annual returns. It will use charts, graphs, and tables to communicate key financial data.

Fees and Expenses. Every mutual fund has several fees. In some cases, when comparing similar funds from different companies, the choice will be determined by the fees. In this section, pay attention to all of the fees that the investor pays directly and the fees that are paid from the fund's assets (such as the management fee). In this section you can determine if a fund is *loaded* or not.

LOAD A fee or commission charged to an investor who buys or redeems shares in a mutual fund. The fee charged upon buying is called a *front-end* load and the fee charged on redeeming is called a *back-end* load.

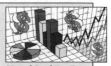

Mutual Fund Key Term

LOADED FUND A mutual fund that charges fees.

FRONT-END LOAD A fee or commission charged to an investor who buys shares in a mutual fund.

BACK-END LOAD A fee or commission charged to an investor who redeems shares in a mutual fund.

CONSTANT LOAD An ongoing (annual) fee charged to an investor as long as he or she holds shares in a mutual fund. This can be in addition to a

---

front-end load and/or back-end load as well as fees associated with the fund's expense ratio.

NO-LOAD FUND A mutual fund that charges no fee or sales commissions for buying or selling shares.

Warning

COMMISSIONS AND LOSSES When you pay a sales commission for mutual fund shares, you're starting off with a financial loss that you will need to recoup through returns from the fund. In general, loaded funds do not make up for their fees by performing better than no-load funds. They also do not employ more qualified fund managers or offer better customer service than no-load funds. Thus, many investment advisors will recommend staying away from loaded funds. To avoid these funds, watch for the following terms in a fund's prospectus: "12b-1 fees," "front-end load," "back-end load," "deferred load," "front-end sales charge," "back-end sales charge," and "deferred sales charge."

Fund Details. Within the main body of the prospectus, you'll often see more detail about the fund's overall investment strategies and other information of interest to investors.

Shareholder Information. This section of the prospectus explains, in detail, how to buy and sell shares of the fund. Not surprisingly, this is usually the easiest to understand and most straightforward section of the prospectus. This section will give the fund company's Web site, toll-free phone number(s), and mailing address. One of the fastest and easiest ways to buy and sell mutual fund shares and to manage your portfo-

Investing Tip

MINIMUM INVESTMENT Virtually all mutual funds require a minimum initial purchase. This minimum purchase will be low ($100 to $1,000) if you're investing as part of a retirement account (IRA, Keogh, etc.). Otherwise, many mutual funds require a minimum initial purchase of at least $2,500. There will also be a minimum for subsequent purchases. In most cases, however, this will be between $100 and $250.

lio is online, through the fund company's Web site. Before you can buy shares of a mutual fund, you must establish an account with a mutual fund company or a broker. This process is explained within Chapter 6.

Dividends and Capital Gains Distributions. When a fund earns dividends, interest, and other income from its investments, this income is usually distributed to shareholders (minus expenses) as *dividends*. A fund might also realize capital gains from its investments, which must be distributed to shareholders as *capital gain distributions.* A fund's prospectus will explain how and when dividends and capital gains distributions are paid to shareholders and what payment options are available. For example, the investor can reinvest all of his or her dividends and capital gains, reinvest only the dividends or only the capital gains, or receive cash payments for both. Some mutual fund companies allow for income from one fund to automatically be invested into another fund.

Tax Consequences. Unless you're investing only in tax-free funds, most mutual funds have tax consequences for the shareholders. The tax rules vary greatly if you're investing for retirement. This section of the prospectus will explain what types of taxes shareholders are subject to paying, including federal income tax, state taxes, and/or local taxes.

The Fund's Manager. The performance of a fund is determined greatly by the person (or people) managing it. This person decides how to invest the pooled money of the shareholders and handles the fund's business affairs. The fund manager is responsible for managing the portfolio's assets, which are typically in the millions of dollars, sometimes even in the billions. The experience, education, expertise, and dedication of the fund's manager will directly and dramatically impact a fund's performance. (At the end of this chapter, you'll read an in-depth interview with a mutual fund manager and learn more about their responsibilities.)

Financial Highlights. Composed of financial spreadsheets and tables, this section of a prospectus offers additional financial details about the fund, including a five-year financial history, and tells how this financial information impacts shareholders and the fund's NAV. This financial information is audited by a third party (a public accounting firm), such as PricewaterhouseCoopers, LLP.

The Shareholder Report/Annual Report

In addition to the prospectus, which is primarily written for potential investors, mutual fund companies also publish shareholder reports—quarterly, semi-annual, or annual

Investing Tip

WEB HELP You can download the prospectus for almost any mutual fund by visiting the Yahoo! Finance Free Prospectus service (*yahoo.fundinfo.wilink.com/asp/F130_search_ENG.asp*). For easy reference, funds are listed alphabetically, by fund family, and by investment objective.

reports for each of their funds. These documents contain primarily financial and performance information of direct interest to the fund's shareholders. In some cases, they are longer than the prospectus.

The main sections of a shareholder report or annual report include the following:

- **Letter from the President/Chair.** This is a letter to shareholders from the president or chair of the company.
- **Letter from the Fund Manager.** In the form of a business letter or in a Q&A format, the fund manager shares highlights of the fund's performance and strategies.
- **Recent Fund Performance.** This is a description of how the fund has performed recently, typically with charts, graphs, and tables to show pertinent financial data. At the beginning of the report, this information is summarized. Here, you'll see displayed the fund's average annual total returns for the past year, for the past five years, and over the life of the fund.
- **Shareholder Expenses.** Here you'll find a detailed summary of fees and expenses incurred by the fund that are passed along to shareholders, including management

fees, transaction costs, and other ongoing expenses.

- **Portfolio Holdings.** This is a summary of the fund's primary holdings and will list significant changes to holdings. For example, the annual report for Fidelity's Growth & Income Portfolio Fund (dated June 30, 2006) listed its top ten stocks and the percentage of the fund's net assets invested in each of those stocks at that time and for the prior six-month period. Additional information about the fund's top five market sectors and asset allocation were provided. This was followed by a detailed listing of all the fund's holdings (including the number of shares of each stock and the net value of each holding). At the end of this summary, the fund's total net assets were listed.

- **Financial Statements.** Every shareholder report or annual report also contains detailed financial statements pertaining to the fund, including a Statement of Assets and Liabilities, a Statement of Operations, a Statement of Changes in Net Assets, and Financial Highlights.

- **Footnotes.** This finial section of the report contains legal details relating to the fund, such as a description of accounting and operating policies, information about how fees and expenses are calculated, and a report from the independent accounting firm that audits the fund's financial records. This section might also contain detailed resumes of the members of the fund's management team.

Investing Tips

QUARTERLY REVIEWS Many mutual fund companies publish quarterly or semi-annual reviews pertaining to specific funds.

Six Things to Know About a Fund Before Investing

The following are six key pieces of information you should know before investing in any mutual fund. This is information that you can obtain from the fund's prospectus, from the annual report, and/or through independent research. Mutual fund analyst companies, like Morningstar, also provide summaries of mutual funds that contain these key pieces of information.

1. **Past Performance**—how the fund has performed over the past year, five years, ten years, and the life of the fund.

2. **Level of Risk**—how much risk the investor takes on and the types of risk associated with the fund.

3. **Holdings**—what type of holdings the fund has, including its asset allocation, level of diversification, and primary investment strategies.

4. **Manager**—who manages the fund and how experienced, educated, and qualified he or she is.

5. **Costs and Fees**—how much it costs to buy and sell shares of the fund and what fees are associated with owning the fund.

6. **Analyst Ratings**—what third-party analysts think about

the fund. As you'll discover, there are many criteria used to analyze and rank mutual funds, based upon their performance over time, how they perform compared with similar funds with a similar investment strategies, how they perform compared with all other mutual funds, and how they perform compared with the market as a whole, an index, or another benchmark.

By reviewing these six primary pieces of information about any mutual fund, the average investor will obtain enough insight to make intelligent investment decisions.

Analyzing the Costs and Fees

Before making an investment, it's essential that you know all of the fees you'll be required to pay and calculate how these expenses will impact your investment and your progress toward your financial goals immediately and over time. For example, if a fund has a high expense ratio and your time horizon is ten, 20, or 30 years, those fees will add up over time.

The following is a brief summary of the costs and fees associated with investing in mutual funds. Not all of these fees apply to all funds and the amounts of these fees vary greatly. You can save money by shopping for high-ranked, well-performing funds with low fees.

Sales commission (load). This is a fee you may have to pay to buy or sell fund shares, for the broker (at least in theory). Funds that charge a sales commission are called *loaded* funds.

Transaction fees. These are the fees you pay to the mutual fund company to buy, sell, or transfer shares, fees that go into the fund's portfolio.

Purchase fee. This fee applies when you purchase shares of a fund. It's not a font-end sales load because it's paid to the fund (not to a broker) and is typically imposed to defray some of the fund's costs associated with the purchase.

Redemption fee. This fee applies when you sell (redeem) shares of the fund.

Account maintenance fees. These fees are paid out of the fund's assets and cover the fund's management fees and any expenses associated with operating and maintaining the fund. You do not pay these fees, but they impact a fund's return on investment. All mutual funds charge these fees, but the fees vary from fund to fund. To know what it costs every year to be invested in a mutual fund, check out the expense ratio. As explained in Chapter 1, this is an annual calculation of the percentage of the fund's assets that is spent paying expenses for the year, including 12b-1 fees, management fees, administrative costs, operating expenses, and all other ongoing expenses associated with the operation of the fund. These are fees that are incurred for owning shares in a fund. By looking at the expense ratio of a fund over the years, you can determine if the fund is becoming more expensive to own.

Finally—taxes. This is money you pay to the government, not to brokers or the mutual fund company. However, the taxes you

12B-1 FEES The percent of a mutual fund's assets assessed for marketing and distribution expenses, such as advertising, dealer compensation, and printing and mailing prospectuses and informational brochures. The amount of the fee is stated in the fund's prospectus.

Mutual Fund Key Term

pay as a result of your investment impact your return on investment and you should calculate them into your costs.

Exchange-Traded Funds: An Alternative to Mutual Funds

Exchange-traded funds (ETFs) are a relatively new investment, dating back only to 1989. Investors can use ETFs as an alternative to open-ended index funds; ETFs are in some ways like closed-end funds. ETFs are somewhat like index funds and somewhat like stocks.

Like index funds, most ETFs attempt to mimic the performance of major indexes, such as the S&P 500, Dow Jones Industrial Average (DJIA), or NASDAQ 100, or focus on a specific industry or sector. Like stocks, ETFs are traded on the

OPEN-END(ED) FUND A mutual fund for which the number of shares available to investors is unlimited. Most mutual funds are open-end funds.

Mutual Fund Key Term

CLOSED-END(ED) FUND A mutual fund in which the fund manager has limited the number of shares. Unlike open-ended mutual funds, closed-end funds do not redeem their shares. The shares of a closed-end fund trade on the open securities market.

major stock exchanges. As a result, the per-share price of an ETF will fluctuate throughout the day, like the price of a stock and unlike the value of a mutual fund, which is calculated as an NAV at the end of a business day. Because ETFs are traded on stock exchanges, investors must work through brokers, just as they would to trade shares of stocks. Because ETFs are treated like stocks, investors can sell them short, use a limit order, buy on margin, or take advantage of a stop-loss order.

One benefit to ETFs is that the fees associated with them are typically lower than with index funds and there is typically no minimum initial purchase. Broker fees, however, apply when purchasing or redeeming shares of an ETF. Depending on how they're used, ETFs can also be more tax-efficient than index funds; however, this is an issue that you'll want to review with your accountant.

Some of the major issuers of ETFs are Barclays Global Investors, State Street Global Advisors, Vanguard Group, Rydex Financial Services, PowerShares, and WisdomTree.

For more information about ETFs, you can visit the following Web sites:

- **Barclays Global Investors (iShares)**—*www.ishares.com*
- **ETF.com**—*www.exchangetradedfunds.com*
- **PowerShares**—*www.powershares.com*
- **U.S. Securities and Exchange Commission**—
  www.sec.gov/answers/etf.htm
- **Vanguard**—*https://flagship.vanguard.com/VGApp/hnw/ FundsVIPER*

Many independent investment analyst companies—including Morningstar, A.G. Edwards, Morgan Stanley, and Merrill Lynch—publish comprehensive data and research on ETFs. In September 2006, Morningstar launched a monthly publication, *ETFInvestor* (800 608-9570, *www.morningstar.com/ Products/Store_ETFInvestor.html*) ($109.00 per year). This publication includes detailed data on 150 of the largest and most widely held ETFs, plus ongoing investment tips and strategies for effectively incorporating ETFs into your portfolio. Like mutual funds, ETFs are *not* insured by the FDIC.

Investing Tip

FOR MORE INFORMATION For a listing of ETFs—complete with ticker symbol, "style box," and information on returns—visit *www.morningstar.com/ Cover/ETF.html* and click on "View complete list."

Advice from an Expert: Larry J. Puglia, Fund Manager

One of the biggest advantages of mutual funds is that your money, when pooled with the funds of thousands of other investors, gets managed by a professional fund manager. A fund manager is someone with proven experience, expertise, education, and skills who is responsible for managing millions (often billions) of dollars on behalf of a fund's shareholders.

In this interview, you'll hear from Larry J. Puglia, a mutual fund manager for T. Rowe Price, who manages the company's well-known and successful Blue Chip Growth Fund.

Puglia is a graduate of the University of Notre Dame with a degree in accounting and finance, but that's only the start of his extremely impressive resume. Puglia is a Certified Public Accountant (CPA) who spent years auditing large companies from a wide range of industries. He later went back to school to earn his M.B.A. from the University of Virginia, with the goal of getting involved in investment management. Puglia was hired by T. Rowe Price in 1990 as an analyst. In 1993, when the Blue Chip Growth Fund was created, Puglia was recruited as the fund's manager, a position he's held ever since. The fund was initially seeded with $2 million, but has grown over the years to now have assets in excess of $16 billion.

Please describe the T. Rowe Price Blue Chip Growth Fund.

Larry J. Puglia: "It was designed to be a quality growth fund with a focus on companies with durable and sustainable earnings. We look for companies with leading market positions—those that are number one or two in their industry in terms of market share. We also look for companies with seasoned management and with strong financial fundamentals. The product is designed to hold all-season growth companies, which we believe can perform reasonably well in all economic environments.

"Because this is a conservative growth fund that is well diversified and tends to focus on companies that can compound earnings for our clients, it is well suited for retirement accounts or as a general-purpose growth product that tends to have a little less of an aggressive profile than most growth funds. We generally perform very well when benchmarked against the S&P 500 and better than other large-cap growth products."

As the fund's manager, what are your primary responsibilities?

Larry J. Puglia: "Above all, my responsibility is to construct a portfolio that is well diversified and comprised of high-quality growth companies where we think the risk/reward is in our favor. This involves a lot of different responsibilities, starting with having a very clear idea of the investment objectives, the risk constraints, and the suitability of particular investments. In a nutshell, I hold the role of a gatekeeper. I must understand what types of investments are suitable for the product, and then make sure the product is comprised of those investments.

"I work very closely with investment analysts within our firm. As an experienced analyst myself, and with the help of other analysts, we identify suitable investments. There are no two more important aspects of my job than finding companies that meet our qualitative standard and that are valued so they give us a reasonably good chance of generating strong investment results.

"Other aspects of my job involve meeting with clients and perspective clients, making presentations to shareholders, and preparing semi-annual reports that go to shareholders. There's also a marketing element to my job, which involves being interviewed by the media, but that's something I typically do at the end of the day, after the markets have closed.

"One of the things I am a stickler for and that I feel strongly about is spending at least 80 percent of my time doing investment analysis, constructing and managing portfolios. Almost every morning, I will look at raw news items from every company the fund owns or is looking to own. I also need to sift through up to 300 e-mails and voice mails per day that contain information related to the fund from a wide range of sources. This takes up at least two to four hours per day.

"Each day, I'll also be involved with several in-person or telephone meetings with top-level executives from the companies our fund holds or that we're actively researching. I'll also spend time, when appropriate, visiting companies firsthand, meeting with the CEO, CFO, head of research, and the director of marketing, for example. On-site visits are a big part of the rigorous analysis we do. I personally like to do my trading in the afternoon, after I have been able to assimilate the day's new information."

In general, why do you believe that mutual funds are such an attractive investment?

Larry J. Puglia: "Mutual funds give investors a vehicle that is well diversified, relatively low-cost and tax-efficient, plus if it's managed well, it should provide above-average, risk-adjusted performance over time. People can get started with ease, investing a small amount of money, plus get above-average performance if the fund is well managed."

When an investor is evaluating a mutual fund, what should he or she look for?

Larry J. Puglia: "The same things I look for before investing in companies. One of the most important things to look at is the fund's management team. Look for honest, competent people, who have a demonstrated track record of achievement. Before that, however, the investor should carefully evaluate their investment needs and objectives. They also need to understand their time horizon and return expectations, plus decide on appropriate asset allocation for their portfolio as a whole. This will help the investor better select investments that can satisfy their needs.

"I recommend investing with a company, like T. Rowe Price, that has a reputation for doing extensive research and analysis. The portfolio management team managing a fund should follow a methodology that has proven itself over time. This means that the fund's management manages risk well and generates above-average, risk-adjusted returns. I have seen many people make poor investment decisions because they've selected investments that were not managed properly or that didn't utilize an investment methodology with a proven track record. The research, analysis, and support behind the fund are very important."

Is there anything specific an investor should look for in a mutual fund's prospectus?

Larry J. Puglia: "The prospectus is important because it tells you who will be managing your money, how it will be managed, how it will be invested, and what investment strategies will be used. I would emphasize that as valuable as I think the prospectus is, you need to be comfortable with the fund's management team and have confidence in their ability to manage the portfolio in a way that is consistent with the investor's objectives and risk tolerance. Reading a fund's semi-annual or annual reports and other communiqués is important. These documents showcase what the fund has done over time in terms of performance results."

Do you recommend that investors use third-party analysis tools when selecting mutual funds?

Larry J. Puglia: "Yes. These can be helpful tools. However, the investor needs to be careful. Some analytical tools don't necessarily provide the insight an investor can best utilize. The investor should have complete confidence in the quality of the analytical information they rely on. I am always careful about endorsing products, but I have respect for Morningstar and Standard & Poor's. These firms have substantive things to say with their analysis. These products do not replace the need to carefully read a fund's prospectus and annual reports, however."

What are some of the biggest mistakes made by mutual fund investors?

Larry J. Puglia: "The most prevalent mistake is that investors tend to chase positive past performance and hot trends."

Do you have any tips for dealing with risk?

Larry J. Puglia: "Every mutual fund has a generated track record for its volatility. This is something you can look at when evaluating its potential risk. If a fund lacks proper diversification or has poor management, it can become very risky. Sector or industry funds and emerging market funds tend to have significant risk associated with them."

Is there any other mutual fund investment advice you'd like to share?

Larry J. Puglia: "Investors should be diligent and thorough when choosing their investment objectives and risk tolerance. Once you've established your portfolio, check on it periodically to make sure everything is being managed in a way you thought it would be. If it is, be patient, especially if the fund is performing well compared to other products in its class. One common mistake is that investors pull out of a fund too quickly if expectations aren't immediately met."

Research Your Funds

This chapter has helped you better understand how mutual funds work and how you can use them to achieve your financial objectives. The next chapter focuses on how to research and learn about specific mutual funds. You'll discover tools that can be used to perform some of your analysis and research, plus learn how to use the vast resources of the top analytical companies, like Morningstar, to help you choose specific mutual funds to add to your portfolio.

CHAPTER 5

Researching
Mutual Funds

WHAT'S IN THIS CHAPTER

- ■ Why research is important and what you'll learn
- ■ How to conduct research and what to analyze
- ■ Sources of current price quotes and performance data
- ■ An interview with an independent mutual fund analyst

A t the same time this book was being written, the NBC television network introduced a new series, called *Heroes*. It's about a group of ordinary adults from around the world who suddenly acquire superpowers. Wouldn't it be great if this were based on reality and that people like you and me could develop psychic abilities? Think about how much of an advantage this would offer when making investments! Using psychic abilities, an investor would know, without a doubt, exactly what investment opportunities to pursue in order to get rich.

Well, since we don't have superpowers and since even the so-called real-life psychics haven't been able to fine-tune their powers enough to predict the performance of the stock market, we're stuck doing research and making educated guesses when it comes to deciding what mutual funds and other investments to use.

As you know, a lot of things affect how a mutual fund performs. Among other things, it has to do with the management team, the asset allocation, the holdings, how the market is performing as a whole, timing, and the fees.

Most people choose to establish their investment portfolio using mutual funds because these investment products allow investors to rely on someone else's expertise. Mutual funds also enable investors to create well-diversified portfolios with minimal effort and not have to spend a lot of time overseeing their portfolios.

But out of the thousands of mutual funds, which handful of funds should you invest in? To answer this question, perform your own research, use the research offered by third parties, and/or consult with an investment advisor.

This leads to the next question. What kind of research and how much research are required to make intelligent mutual fund investment decisions? Well, that's what this chapter covers. Fortunately, you don't have to be a financial wizard or spend countless hours crunching numbers in order to make smart investment decisions. This is because independent mutual fund analysts and the financial experts who manage the various funds have already done much of the complex work for you. All you need to do is read (and hopefully understand) their findings and then determine how their conclusions and advice, based on their analysis and research, relate to your investment goals.

If you use a *fund selector tool*, which can be found on many personal finance and investment-oriented Web sites, you

Investing Tip

DO YOUR HOMEWORK You should research not only individual funds, but also how the funds in your portfolio will work together to achieve your investment objectives. For example, a fund may be highly ranked and offer excellent returns over the long term, but if your time horizon is less than five years you might not benefit from what the fund offers. You also don't want the funds in your portfolio to overlap much in their focus or with their holdings, or your diversification is reduced.

answer a few basic questions about the type of fund(s) you want and then have the tool narrow down the thousands of mutual funds to a handful that meet your criteria. Then, you can access analytical and research information on those specific funds in order to make smart decisions about which ones to invest in. The process of picking the right mutual funds and creating a well-rounded portfolio takes anywhere from just a few minutes to a few hours—if you know what information to rely on and which tools to use.

FUND SELECTOR (SCREENER) A type of online tool that searches through the 14,000-plus mutual funds to find those that meet whichever criteria the user has chosen, based on type, performance, risk, ratings, fund manager 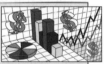 **Mutual Fund Key Term** tenure, fees charged, or other factors. Free tools offer a few dozen search options, while some of the premium, fee-based tools offer 60 or more screening options, plus screens designed by experts to meet specific objectives.

Why Research Is Important

Once you pinpoint the type of fund you wish to invest in, say a blue-chip (large-cap) growth fund or an index fund modeled after the S&P 500, there are numerous similar funds from which to choose. You must figure out which fund would fit best within your portfolio, based on your goals, time horizon, and risk tolerance—not trends or marketing.

Even just the most basic research, which involves reading the fund's prospectus and most recent shareholder report or going online to obtain independent analysis of a fund, will prove helpful when choosing specific funds.

Whenever you invest in a mutual fund, stock, bond, or any other type of investment, you're in a sense betting that the value of that investment will rise over time (within your time horizon) at a rate greater than the rate of inflation and provide you a better return than other types of investments. In essence, the investment decisions you make are guesses about the future.

As an investor, you can make guesses based on hunches, psychic visions, or "hot tips" you receive from a friend—*or* you can make educated guesses based on research you perform and the reliable, current, and accurate research data you collect from various sources. Again, doing even minimal research before you invest your money will help you make more intelligent decisions. Thanks to the Internet, performing research on specific funds takes minutes, not hours. Once you obtain the research information, it may take you time to understand it and put it into context, but that's time well spent.

It's obviously impossible to accurately predict, 100 percent of the time, how any mutual fund will perform. You can, however, look at things like past performance, the qualifications and experience of the manager, the investment strategy, the risk level, the fees, and other pertinent information and then decide whether you believe the fund has a good chance of making you money during the time horizon when you plan to have your money invested.

You can also decide if a specific fund will fit nicely into your portfolio, based on your target asset allocation, and if it will help to balance your holdings and help you achieve your financial goals. One common mistake investors make is to buy funds that have similar holdings. This reduces the diversification of their portfolio and often means paying unnecessary fees for funds they don't really need. Look at the primary holdings of your funds and determine if there's any overlap and, if so, how much. An easy way to do this is to use an online-based *fund comparison tool*, which will be described shortly.

The more you know about a particular fund, its investment strategy, and its holdings, the more able you are to make better decisions. Again, you don't need to invest countless hours in order to obtain the right information needed to make intelligent mutual fund investments.

Warning

CHOOSING ON PAST PEFORMANCE One of the biggest mistakes mutual fund investors make is choosing funds based almost exclusively on past performance. Past performance is never an indication of future performance. Plus, funds that have performed extremely well for a while are often destined to experience a cooling off period.

What You Can Learn from Researching Funds

Basically, what you should learn from the research you perform or the research you acquire should focus only on the information you need in order to feel comfortable about the investment decisions you make. It's very easy to over-analyze an investment opportunity and gather too much information or irrelevant data that will only cloud your judgment.

In Chapter 4, you learned about the six things to know about a mutual fund before you should invest in it:

1. Past Performance
2. Level of Risk
3. Fund Holdings
4. Fund Manager
5. Costs and Fees
6. Analyst Ratings

Investing Tip

Other things to consider when evaluating a fund are the stability and reputation of the mutual fund company and the fund's compatibility with your investment goals. Also, consider how the fund will alter the asset allocation of your portfolio.

As you research specific mutual funds, these six pieces of information about each fund will be the most useful to you, especially if you're a novice. Some of this information can be found quickly, simply by reading the fund's prospectus and the most recent shareholder report. You can also use information from an independent mutual fund analyst company, such as Morningstar, which provides all of this key information summarized on a single sheet of paper or a computer screen.

Warning

KNOW YOUR SOURCES Before relying on any research or information about a mutual fund (or any other investment opportunity), make sure you know the source of the information. Determine if the information is accurate, reliable, and current. Information in a fund's prospectus or shareholder report is accurate and reliable; it's also reviewed and audited by an independent third-party. If you're relying on outside information and opinions, from analysts and investment advisors, for example, it's important to know their qualifications, understand their methods for doing research and analysis, and decide how much faith you want to put in their recommendations and conclusions. There are countless Web sites, magazines, and newsletters that offer mutual fund investing advice, research, and analysis. It's important to choose the right sources of information to rely upon.

Narrow Your Search Using a Fund Selection Tool

A free, online fund selection tool can help you quickly narrow down your choices from the 14,000-plus mutual funds. There are two types of fund selection (screener) tools—those offered by mutual fund companies that will help you choose from among their funds only and those offered by independent organizations that maintain a vast database of mutual funds from many companies.

For example the Fund Evaluator℠ on the Fidelity.com Web site (*personal.fidelity.com/research/funds/index.html*) will help you choose among the mutual funds offered by Fidelity Investments. To use this tool, you make four choices to set your criteria. First, choose an investment category; the 70 choices are based on what each fund owns. Then, select past perform-ance—a time span (year-to-date, one year, three years, five years, or ten years) and a return percentage (0 percent or greater, 5 percent or greater, 10 percent or greater, 15 percent or greater, or 20 percent or greater). Finally, choose a Morningstar star rating (between one and five stars or "no preference"). Based on your criteria, the Fund Evaluator^{SM} will give you details about a handful of appropriate funds. So, instead of having to research hundreds of Fidelity funds in detail, you can focus on those that meet your criteria.

The "advanced search" version of the Fund Evaluator^{SM} enables you to search for the most compatible funds for your portfolio based on additional criteria, including expense ratio, loaded funds or no-load funds, fund management tenure, net assets of the fund, and risk/volatility. You can select only the search options that are most important to you.

Many mutual fund companies offer similar fund selection tools on their Web sites. Morningstar's Web site (*screen.morn-ingstar.com/FundSelector.html*) offers a free Fund Screener that contains detailed information about thousands of funds from all of the mutual fund companies. If you subscribe to the com-pany's premium service, you can instantly learn about the funds this tool recommends and instantly compare funds based on criteria you select. To use the Fund Screener, begin by selecting a Fund Group (selecting from stock or bond funds, by Morningstar category, and/or by fund manager tenure) and Cost and Purchase (selecting by minimum initial investment, between load and no-load funds, and/or by expense ratio). The Fund Screener also allows you to screen funds based on Morningstar Star Ratings, risk, and/or returns (year-to-date, one year, three years, five years, or ten years). For stock funds, you can further narrow your search based on turnover, total asset value, and/or average market cap. For bond funds, you can further narrow your search based on average credit quality and duration.

You can choose which of these search criteria you want to use and then pinpoint suitable funds in seconds. For example, you can quickly obtain a list of five-star, no-load, blue chip (large-cap) growth funds with an expense ratio below one percent. This broad-type search will result in many matches. You can then add search criteria to further narrow the list of potentially suitable funds. For example, you can look for funds with a manager who has been on the job at least ten years, a minimum initial investment of $3,000 or less, and year-to-date returns greater than or equal to the fund category average.

You'll find additional mutual fund screeners at various investing-related Web sites. Each offers a database containing details about thousands of funds. The criteria by which you can narrow down your search will vary from tool to tool. Here are just a few online fund selection tools:

- **CNN Money Mutual Fund Screener**—
  money.cnn.com/data/funds/screener
- **Forbes Fund Screener**—
  www.forbes.com/finance/screener/Screener.jhtml

Investing Tip

THE FUND SCREENER In addition to its Fund Finder, SmartMoney offers a Fund Screener, which is a premium (fee-based) service that offers the same level of search functionality as Morningstar's premium-based Fund Screener. SmartMoney offers a two-week free trial of its Fund Screener, through *https://ecommerce.smartmoney.com/ecommerce/login*. This premium service features a database of over 14,000 mutual funds and enables investors to search using up to 60 criteria, including performance, risk, and ratings.

- **SmartMoney Fund Finder—** *www.smartmoney.com/fundfinder*
- **Yahoo! Finance Mutual Fund Screener—** *screen.yahoo.com/funds.html*

Once you've narrowed down your search to between three and five funds that meet your criteria and that are compatible with your investing goals, you can sit down and carefully read the prospectus and shareholder report for each of those funds and/or use the analytical and research resources offered by a third-party company, such as Morningstar. You want to learn about each fund and gather information in the primary six categories that should be of interest to you—past performance, level of risk, fund holdings, fund manager, costs and fees, and analyst ratings.

Other Useful Research and Analytical Tools

After using a fund selection tool, you can use a fund comparison tool, which will allow you to place several mutual funds side by side to compare things like performance, ratings, fees, and risk. This type of tool is extremely helpful for evaluating similar funds and for choosing one from among them.

For example, if you were interested in comparing Fidelity's Blue Chip Growth Fund with Fidelity's Blue Chip Value Fund, you could use the Compare Funds tool offered at the Fidelity.com Web site (*personal.fidelity.com/research/funds/index.html*) and enter the two ticker symbols (FBGRX and FBCVX).

The Compare Funds tool will display an on-screen table, listing side by side information and data about these two funds. With one additional click of the mouse on the name of a fund, you can obtain a graph showing cumulative fund performance for the period of time you specify (year-to-date, one year, three years, five years, or ten years). The data table and graph will give you information, such as the following:

- Investment objectives
- Morningstar category
- Assets
- Morningstar Star Rating
- Performance (non-load adjusted returns) for year-to-date, one year, three years, five years, and ten years
- Expense ratio
- Turnover rate percentage
- Transaction fees
- Volatility (risk) measures (including *Beta*, R^2, and *Standard Deviation*)

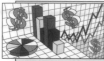

Mutual Fund Key Term

BETA A measure of a fund's or a stock's risk (volatility) relative to the market or another benchmark. The benchmark index has a beta of 1.0. A beta above 1.0 indicates that a fund's returns have fluctuated more than the benchmark index; a beta of below 1.0 indicates less fluctuation than the benchmark.

R^2 A measure of how closely performance of a fund or a stock correlates with the performance of a benchmark index, expressed as a number between 0.00 and 1.00. An R^2 of 1.00 indicates a perfect correlation: all of the fluctuations of the fund or the stock match fluctuations of the index. An R^2 of 0.00 indicates that there's no correlation. If a fund had an R^2 of .47 relative to its benchmark, it would mean that 47 percent of its fluctuations match fluctuations in the benchmark. The lower the R^2, the greater the performance gap between the fund or the stock and the index; in other words, the more the fund or the stock reacts according to factors other than the factors that influence the market as measured by that benchmark.

STANDARD DEVIATION A measure of the variability of a fund's or a stock's returns over a period of time. The higher the standard deviation, the greater the variability. The calculation of standard deviation does not distinguish between gains and losses: it measures absolute variability, the degree of movement above or below the mean.

On the Web sites of many mutual fund companies and personal finance and investor-related Web sites, you'll find a collection of other online tools that are useful to mutual fund investors, including:

- **Asset Allocator**—This tool will help you quickly determine what combination of fund types (and any other investments) will provide you with the best chance of meeting your investment goals without incurring unnecessary risk.

- **Portfolio Allocator**—This tool will help you manage your asset allocation and test what could happen if you added or subtracted funds. This is useful for asking "what if?" questions about mutual fund investments. For example, you could determine what would happen to your asset allocation if you added a specific index fund or emerging markets fund.

- **Portfolio Manager**—This tool enables you to more easily manage all of the investments in your portfolio. (This tool is described in detail in Chapter 7.)

- **Risk Analyzer**—This tool enables you to analyze the level of risk for the specific funds and other investments in your portfolio or funds you're considering adding. You can also see how your portfolio might perform if market conditions change.

- **Cost Analyzer**—This tool allows you to compare the costs and fees of specific funds. For example, you can see the impact of fees on your portfolio's value over a specified number of years, depending on whether you added one particular fund or a similar fund.

Tools and Publications Offered by Morningstar

Morningstar, Inc. (*www.morningstar.com*) is an independent investment research company based in Chicago. The company has been analyzing mutual funds since 1984. Morningstar is the most comprehensive, respected, trusted, and widely used source of independent mutual fund analysis and research information.

One reason why so many investors rely on analysis and research performed by Morningstar is because the company's analysts take highly complex data and make it easily understandable to novice investors. The pertinent information on any specific fund is provided in a concise, easy-to-read, one- or two-page report. This information is then put into perspective through recommendations, articles, and reports, also written by expert analysts using easy-to-understand terminology—unlike the prospectus and shareholder reports for many mutual funds, which are typically filled with technical jargon.

For each of thousands of mutual funds, Morningstar issues a "star rating" of between one and five stars. This rating alone can be a valuable tool for deciding whether or not to invest in a fund. The analysts at Morningstar rate each fund according to its relative performance within more than 40 well-defined fund categories and then calculates its risk-adjusted performance compared with other funds with similar objectives. In other words, blue-chip stock growth funds are compared with other blue-chip stock growth funds, so the investor can compare a handful of similar funds within a specific category. Star ratings focus on past performance and are just one factor to consider when evaluating a fund.

Mutual Funds: A Quick-Start Guide

The Morningstar FundInvestor 500 is a publication that summarizes the analysis and research about the top 500 mutual funds that Morningstar recommends. The monthly *FundInvestor* newsletter keeps this information up-to-date. Within these publications, investors can find "Analyst Picks," which are two-page, detailed spotlights about particular funds, and one-page summaries about 500 funds that Morningstar analysts consider to be the best. Similar information is also available for exchange-traded funds, stocks, and other types of investments.

For each fund, the Morningstar staff researches information about management, strategy, costs, stewardship, and performance. The *FundInvestor* book, the newsletters, and the company's Web site consolidate information about individual mutual funds onto a single page. From text, tables, and a few graphic icons, plus its famous Style Box, investors can obtain the core information they should know about a fund before investing in it as well as the proprietary rankings, grades, and analytical summaries created by the Morningstar analysts.

A single page shows dozens of key pieces of information about a fund, including name, ticker symbol, load, NAV, total assets, category, investment style, performance history, performance analysis, risk analysis, asset allocation (composition), sector breakdown of holdings (including weightings), details about fees, Morningstar Star Rating, current investment style (Style Box), and a few paragraphs by one of the company's analysts who summarizes Morningstar's take on the fund.

MORNINGSTAR STYLE BOX™ A graphic representation of a mutual fund in terms of three investment styles (small-cap stocks, mid-cap stocks, large-cap stocks) and three **Mutual Fund Key Term** objectives (growth, value, blend—both growth and value), forming a matrix of nine cells, one of which is highlighted. The Style Box characterizes a fund in one of nine ways: small-cap value, small-cap blend, small-cap growth, mid-cap value, mid-cap blend, mid-cap growth, large-cap value, large-cap blend, and large-cap growth. Thus, for example, if the middle cell of the Style Box is highlighted, it means that the fund consists mainly of mid-cap stocks with a combination value/growth focus. If the upper-left cell of the Style Box is highlighted, it means that the fund's primary holdings are in large-cap, value-oriented stocks, such as blue-chip stocks.

To learn more about the many tools, publications, and other resources Morningstar offers to mutual fund investors, visit the Morningstar Web site. You can begin by using the free information and tools or take advantage of a free, two-week trial of the site's premium services.

Premium Membership is priced at $14.95 per month (or $135.00 for a year). This gives you instant and unlimited access to all of the Web site's tools, analysis, and research data. You can also subscribe (for a fee) to any of the company's publications.

Sources of Current Quotes and Financial Data

If you'll be using a portfolio management tool that doesn't automatically obtain current mutual fund price quotes from the Internet, you can obtain these quotes from a wide range of

Warning

INSTANT X-RAY TOOL The Morningstar Instant X-Ray (*portfolio.morn-ingstar.com/NewPort/Free/InstantXRayDEntry.aspx*) is an online tool that looks at your entire portfolio of mutual funds and allows you to better understand its basic characteristics at a glance. The tool will evaluate your asset allocation, exposure to different investment styles, and other important factors. To use this tool, simply enter for each fund the ticker symbol and the dollar value of your shares or the percentage of your allocation. In seconds, you'll receive a summary of your asset allocation (in the form of a pie chart), a sector-by-sector breakdown of your holdings, a summary of fees and expenses, a world map showing where your portfolio has investments, a Morningstar Style Box that shows your diversification based on valuation, and an overall performance comparison between your funds and the S&P 500.

online and printed sources, including the following:

- **CNNMoney.com**—*money.cnn.com*
- **FundEstimate.com**—*www.fundestimate.com*
- *Investor's Business Daily* (printed or online edition, *www.investors.com*)
- **Morningstar**—*www.morningstar.com*
- **MSN Money**—*moneycentral.msn.com/home.asp*
- *The Wall Street Journal* (printed or online edition, *www.wsj.com*)
- **Yahoo! Finance**—*finance.yahoo.com*

In addition to mutual fund price quotes, many of the popular investment-related Web sites, including Forbes.com (*www.forbes.com/funds/BestWorst.jhtml*), offer listings of the best- and worst-performing funds for specific time periods. *Forbes* magazine and the magazine's Web site also publish an annual "Honor Roll" directory of funds it recommends and semiannual evaluations of 2,500 funds. Like Morningstar's data and recommendations, the information published by *Forbes* comes from an independent third party.

Some of the tools mentioned within this chapter and many of the fund manager tools described in Chapter 7 enable you to chart or graph data, for a visual representation of information that is often easier to understand than a table containing columns of numbers, especially when you're comparing funds or reviewing the holdings of a particular fund or several funds.

Investing Tips

DIVERSIFICATION Remember: a well-diversified portfolio consists of stocks, bonds, and money market investments. Several stock funds and bond funds can provide ample diversity. When considering stock funds, check the investment style (growth vs. income) and the risk. Funds invest primarily in small-cap U.S. stocks are riskier than funds focusing on blue-chip (large-cap) stocks. International investments, especially in emerging markets, can increase diversification, but also increase risk.

DON'T ALWAYS PLAY IT SAFE When it comes to risk, playing it safe does not always save you money. While you could invest all of your money in a money market account, a savings account, or CDs, for example, which are virtually guaranteed to offer a positive return, over time the rate of inflation tends to be higher than the return of these very safe investments. So, over ten or 20 years, for example, you could actually lose money with super-safe investments. Your goal should be, at the very least, to seek returns over the long term that beat inflation and compensate you for the fees you'll be paying. In a ten-year period, for example, an inflation rate of three percent could reduce your money's purchasing power by as much as 26 percent.

Advice from an Expert: Christine Benz, Mutual Fund Analyst

Christine Benz is the director of mutual fund analysis at Morningstar, the world's most respected source of independent mutual fund research data. She has been working as an analyst since 1996, but has been employed by Morningstar for over 13 years. She has also served as editor of several of the company's publications, including *FundInvestor*.

Morningstar's 28 mutual fund analysts constantly review over 2,000 funds and provide readers with recommendations. The analysts use a set of proprietary tools to evaluate each fund on its own merits. Then each fund is compared with other funds in its peer group. An analyst might also interview the fund manager to get a sense of a fund's long-term strategy and current position. Morningstar also looks at the expenses and fees for each fund.

What are some of the services Morningstar offers to individual investors?

Christine Benz: "Our company's roots are in mutual funds and mutual fund analysis; however, we've branched out in recent years. We also now cover over 1,500 individual stocks, as well as exchange-traded funds and hedge funds. Morningstar's primary tools for individual investors can be found on the Morningstar.com Web site. We also offer a wide range of printed publications and newsletters. Pretty much anything that falls under the category of financial research is something Morningstar is somehow involved in providing."

Mutual Fund Key Term

HEDGE FUND A fund that is managed aggressively to get the highest returns by using derivatives and swaps, selling short, and working with other strategies. The funds typically attract investors with high net worth and institutions.

What are some of the tools on the Morningstar Web site?

Christine Benz: "There is a wealth of information available on the site. Investors can find a lot of how-to and educational articles. We also provide plenty of analysis about individual mutual funds and related financial data. If you know a ticker that's associated with a fund, you can quickly access a vast amount of information about it. This is information that goes well beyond what's published in the fund's prospectus and shareholder report. Basically, any and all information an investor would need in order to decide whether or not to invest in a specific mutual fund is offered on the Morningstar.com Web site."

Is the information on Morningstar.com available free of charge to investors?

Christine Benz: "Some of the information is offered for free. We do have a premium service which investors pay for. It offers access to a vast assortment of additional and extremely powerful investment tools. A lot of the proprietary mutual fund analysis we offer is part of the premium service."

Morningstar is known for its "star ratings" of mutual funds. What is this rating system and how does it work?

Christine Benz: "This is a quantitative measure that attempts to sum up what a fund's past risk-reward profile has been relative to other funds that use a similar investment style. The rating is based half on a fund's returns and half on its risk level, relative to other funds that follow a similar investment strategy. Funds are rated between one and five stars, with five stars representing the highest rating we offer. We usually recommend that investors use the star rating as a starting point for their research. Using our star ratings is a good way to whittle down the large number of funds to a more manageable group when choosing which to invest in."

In your opinion, why are mutual funds such an attractive investment for so many people?

Christine Benz: "Mutual funds offer diversification with a single investment, plus professional management. The drawback to mutual funds is that the fees can add up over time and could wind up costing you more than if you were to buy a basket of individual stocks and then hold on to them for many years. Some mutual fund companies keep a lid on costs and on a fund's expense ratio, while others do not."

Each mutual fund comprises a diversified selection of investments. So, should an investor also seek to diversify his or her funds by focusing on different types and categories of funds?

Christine Benz: "You should, but investors tend to go overboard when it comes to diversification. Once you go beyond ten different mutual funds in your portfolio, you're not doing yourself any favors by adding an eleventh fund. You already have plenty of diversification. Once you go above ten or so funds, you're basically adopting the same investment strategy as a broad market mutual fund would, but you're paying fees to own a bunch of different funds. If someone is first getting started, buying just a few funds is an excellent start. Those funds should, however, be consistent with the goals you're trying to achieve."

How should an investor's strategy differ based on his or her investment goals?

Christine Benz: "If you're saving for a down payment on a new home that you plan to buy within the next two or so years, your time horizon is very short. This means you should invest in less risky investments, such as a money market fund or ultra-short bond fund. In this situation, you want to see very little fluctuation in the value of your principal. If you have a longer time horizon, say ten years or more, you'll probably want to be oriented more to stock funds. You'll see more fluctuation in your principal, but there is more potential for greater gains. Over time, stocks tend to generate higher gains than bonds."

If someone has never invested, what is the best way to get started?

Christine Benz: "This depends on how much time you're willing to spend on this pursuit. If you don't have the time or inclination to learn about investing, paying a financial planner or investment advisor is probably money well spent. But, without a lot of effort, you can dig in and learn a lot quickly, so you can do a lot of your investing yourself."

When evaluating a mutual fund, what does an investor need to consider besides its NAV?

Christine Benz: "There are several key things to look at. First, look at what type of fund it is. Figure out what the fund's strategy is like. This will help you determine if the fund is a good match for you, based on your time horizon, risk tolerance, and goals. Read about the fund's investment strategy and take a look at its holdings. Take a look at the portfolio's manager and see how long they've been on the job. Generally speaking, longer is better. One of the most critical things to look at is a fund's expense ratio. We have found that the expense ratio is a very good predictor of whether or not the fund as a whole will be a good performer. The expense ratio is the fee the fund company charges for managing the investment. This includes the management fee and any administrative costs associated with managing the fund, such as shareholder services."

How important is the mutual fund company an investor chooses?

Christine Benz: "There are great and poor examples of well-known and large mutual fund companies, as well as smaller, lesser-known companies. I think you should go with a company that offers the services you want. It's hard to make a generalization."

You mentioned that the role of a fund manager is important. How should an investor evaluate a fund manager's resume or accomplishments?

Christine Benz: "One thing that I tell investors is to make sure they understand the investment strategy and investment philosophies used by the manager. If the investor understands this, they're more apt to use the fund well. Also, take a look at the resources of the mutual fund company. What resources are backing up the manager? How many analysts does the fund manager have access to?"

When a novice investor looks at some of the Morningstar analytical information, it might be confusing at first. What does an investor need to know about your information?

Christine Benz: "A lot of our analytical reports utilize graphic icons to help communicate information quickly. We typically explain every icon somewhere within the document or report. The investor should understand what everything means, so they can put the information and data in the appropriate context. Our Morningstar Style Box is a common graphic that's used, which an investor should understand.

"One useful tool which can be found on our Web site is the Fund Screener. This asks the investor a few basic questions, and then whittles down the potential list of funds to invest in to a handful that meet their criteria. Funds can be screened very quickly based on category, star rating, and many other criteria. We also offer a free portfolio manager tool, which allows investors to watch over their portfolio on an ongoing basis. This manager displays the portfolio's current value."

What is a Style Box and how does it work?

Christine Benz: "It's a system that shows you what percentage of holdings a specific fund has in specific types of stocks. A Style Box has nine boxes in a grid. It's a quick visual snapshot of how a mutual fund's holdings are distributed. This can be a useful tool for figuring out the investment strategy the manager is using, plus it can be a gauge to measure risk. For example, the bottom-right corner box in a Style Box represents the most risky types of investments. If a lot of your portfolio is clustered in the bottom-right corner of the Style Box, you probably have a lot of risky investments. The upper-left corner of the Style Box tends to represent less risky investments." [More information on understanding the Morningstar Style Boxes is included earlier in this chapter, under "Tools and Publications Offered by Morningstar."]

What are some of the biggest mistakes first-time mutual fund investors often make?

Christine Benz: "The biggest mistake, which is not confined to first-time investors, is chasing performance. This means someone would look down a list of funds and choose the fund with the highest return and then buy that fund with the expectation it will continue to be a good performer. What we have found through our research is that oftentimes high rates of returns are not sustainable. Aside from performance, I would focus more on the fundamental factors of the fund, including its investment strategy, manager, and fees."

What are some of the biggest misconceptions people have about mutual funds?

Christine Benz: "One is that higher costs mean better quality. The costs and fees associated with a mutual fund have very little to do with performance. In fact, the less you pay for a mutual fund, typically the better your returns will be.

The concept that you get what you pay for doesn't carry over into the mutual fund realm."

Do you have any advice for people who are nervous about their mutual fund investments?

Christine Benz: "One reason why people invest in mutual funds is so they can rely on the experienced fund managers to handle the tough investment decisions. Let these people do their job and don't stress out over the day-to-day performance of a fund, especially when you're involved with a long time horizon. Pay attention to giant swings in a fund, for better or worse, but don't worry about small dips."

Is it OK to invest in a mutual fund even if the investor doesn't understand everything in the prospectus or shareholder reports?

Christine Benz: "These documents can be a bit off-putting. They're pretty legalistic. One thing which Morningstar brings to the table is that we put a lot of key information in layperson's terms. I wouldn't be too alarmed if you don't understand everything in a prospectus or shareholder report. After reading these documents, try to come out of the experience with a basic understanding of what the fund is all about, who is managing it, what investment strategies are being used, and what the fees and performance level of the fund are. If you grasp these key concepts, you'll be in good shape."

Do you have any other advice for mutual fund investors?

Christine Benz: "Don't overdiversify by owning shares in too many different mutual funds. Also, watch your costs and fees. Instead of watching your portfolio on a day-to-day basis, I would schedule a few periodic checkups for your portfolio to see how your returns have tracked relative to your targets. I'd also use this checkup as a chance to review your portfolio's asset allocation to make sure it's still on target and in line with your overall financial goals. Once a year, do a thorough, top-to-bottom review of your portfolio and do any asset allocation rebalancing that's necessary.

"I am also a firm believer in *dollar-cost averaging* through automatic investment plans. This instills discipline. This makes good investing sense, because it forces you to invest even if the market is down. Buying mutual fund shares when the market is down is the best time to expand your portfolio."

Mutual Fund Key Term

DOLLAR COST AVERAGING An investment strategy consisting of investing an equal amount of money every month into a fund, regardless of the price of the fund. When the price is lower, the investment buys slightly more shares; when the price is higher, the investment buys slightly fewer shares. This strategy results in lowering the average cost of a share if the price fluctuates up and down. It also decreases the risk of investing a large amount at the wrong time. When you sign up for an automatic investment plan, you'll be using this investment strategy.

It's Time to Start Investing!

Now that you know what to look for when researching and analyzing specific mutual funds, it's time to start investing. The next chapter focuses on opening an account with a mutual fund company and establishing your portfolio. Chapter 7 then focuses on how to properly manage your portfolio using online and software tools and other resources.

CHAPTER 6

Get Started
Investing Now

WHAT'S IN THIS CHAPTER

- Choosing a mutual fund company
- Establishing an account with a mutual fund company
- A listing of well-known mutual fund companies, with contact information
- Setting up your portfolio
- Buying your first mutual fund shares

Mutual Funds: A Quick-Start Guide

Befóre you can invest in mutual funds, you must set up an account with one or more mutual fund companies or a broker who represents several fund companies. If you're setting up a retirement account or *charitable giving* account, the process is slightly more complicated than what's described here, so you'll probably want to work with an investment specialist to set up the accounts appropriately and to make sure you benefit fully from the tax benefits associated with them.

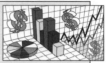

CHARITABLE GIVING Type of investment allowing the investor to make tax-deductible donations with the dividends and capital gains distributions from mutual fund investments and/or donate the value of the investments Mutual Fund Key Term themselves upon death. Many mutual fund companies can help you create a private foundation, make donations anonymously to your favorite charities, and/or donate your money however you choose.

All of the mutual fund companies have retirement planning experts and investment advisors on staff; also, you can hire an independent personal financial planner or accountant to assist you. When you're ready to set up a mutual fund account for general investing purposes, such as for building wealth or saving for college tuition or a home, the process is pretty straightforward, but requires completing some forms, either paper or online.

This chapter will walk you through the basic process of setting up an individual or joint general investing account with any mutual fund company. Once your account is set up and funded, you can begin investing almost immediately.

Choosing Your Mutual Fund Company

Years ago stock brokers exclusively sold stocks, financial planners offered investing advice, and mutual fund companies offered the opportunity to invest in mutual funds. Today, these lines have blurred. Fidelity Investments, Charles Schwab, T. Rowe Price, and countless other companies offer one-stop shops for all of your investing needs.

First and foremost, the mutual fund company you choose to do business with should be well-known, well-established, and highly reputable and offer the services you want and need. The company should understand your needs as an investor and be able to cater to those needs in a way that's easy and convenient for you. This might mean having a customer service office or investment center near your home or office, so you can reap the benefits of in-person advice and service. You might prefer, however, for the company to offer an easy-to-use and easily accessible Web site through which you can manage your account. The fees charged by the mutual fund company should also be a consideration.

The company should offer a vast selection of well-managed funds. Is the company known for its expert analysis, top-notch customer service, and the tools it offers to investors? Companies like Fidelity Investments, Charles Schwab, T. Rowe Price, and Vanguard, for example, each have hundreds of funds and a well-established customer service department that is available in person, by telephone, online, and by mail.

Decide how involved you want to be with your portfolio's management on an ongoing basis and then evaluate the services offered by each company you're considering. Some companies charge less if you'll be doing your own investment and portfolio management. If you're looking for a company that offers extensive support and guidance, would you prefer to interact in person, by telephone, or online? Do you want someone available to assist you 24 hours per day or just during extended business hours? In general, the more services you want and need, the more you'll pay in fees.

Investing Tip

GETTING STARTED Look for a company that offers manageable ongoing balance requirements, low or zero *account maintenance fees*, and initial minimum investments you can afford. If you fall below the required minimum account or fund balance, will you be charged additional fees?

ACCOUNT MAINTENANCE FEES Fees charged by a mutual fund company to set up an account and/or maintain it. There may be a fee if the value of an account or the value of specific investments falls below a specific dollar level. Mutual fund companies will typically waive these account maintenance fees for investors with high-valued portfolios.

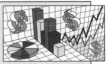

Mutual Fund Key Term

According to Fidelity Investments, for example, once you open a Fidelity account (with a minimum investment of

$2,500), you can choose from over 4,500 Fidelity and non-Fidelity mutual funds, index funds, and exchange-traded funds. Because Fidelity is also a broker, you can invest in individual stocks (for a commission) and use a broad range of online tools to manage your account and portfolio. Customer service assistance is available 24 hours a day and Fidelity operates dozens of investment centers across America where you can receive in-person assistance and support. Not all of the mutual fund companies offer this level of service and support. For example, many companies that offer telephone-based customer service offer it only during extended business hours.

When choosing a mutual fund company, one question to ask is how quickly you can receive your money after you redeem shares in a fund. Also, determine exactly what the process is for doing this. Unless you set up a money wiring option in advance, it could take several days for your shares to be sold and then for

Warning

Determine if the company you're considering also imposes an account set-up fee and/or maintenance fees. If so, determine what these fees will be and how much they'll impact your investment returns. Would it make sense for you to find similar investment opportunities with a company that charges no fees or significantly lower fees? For example, American Century Investments imposes a $12.50 account maintenance fee twice per year if your total investments are less than $10,000. Fidelity Investment charges a Mutual Fund Low Balance Fee of $12.00 per year for each Fidelity fund in which you own under $2,000 worth of shares.

a check to be issued and mailed to your home address. Do requests to sell shares have to be put in writing or will you be able to do this online or by calling a toll-free number?

Ultimately, you want to choose a mutual fund company you can trust and that will provide the tools and resources you need to achieve your investment goals.

Mutual Fund Company Contact Information

The table on the next page gives an alphabetical listing of popular mutual fund companies and contact information. Inclusion within this list is *not* a recommendation or endorsement of any company or any products or services. This contact information will enable you to do the following:

- Learn more about mutual fund and investment products
- Obtain a mutual fund prospectus
- Receive investment advice
- Open an account

Solidifying Your Investment Goals and Plans

Now that you're ready to open an account with a mutual fund company or broker and to start investing, review your investment goals and plans once again. Make sure that the funds you've chosen will allow you to achieve your objectives. You should also consider what other types of investments, if any, you'll use to round out your portfolio.

Company	Address	Phone No.	Web Site
American Century Investments	P.O. Box 419 200Kansas City, MO 64141-6200	(800) 826-8323	www.americancentury.com
Charles Schwab	5190 Neil Road Ste 100 Reno, NV 89502-8532	(866) 232-9890	www.schwab.com
Domini Social Investments	P.O. Box 9785 Providence, RI 02940	(800) 762-6814	www.domini.com
Dreyfus (Mellon)	144 Glenn Curtiss Blvd Uniondale, NY 11556	(888) 782-6620, (800) 337-9339 (800) 323-7023	www.dreyfus.com
Fidelity Investments	P.O. Box 770001 Cincinnati, OH 45277	(800) FIDELITY (343-3548)	www.fidelity.com
Franklin Templeton Investments	P.O. Box 997152 Sacramento, CA 95899	(800) 632-2301	www.franklintempleton. com
Janus Funds	P.O. Box 173375 Denver, CO 80217-3375	(800) 525-3713	www.janus.com
Oppenheimer Funds	P.O. Box 5270 Denver, CO 80217-5270	(888) 470-0862	www.oppenheimerfunds. com
Putnam Investments	P.O. Box 41203 Providence, RI 02940	(800) 225-1581	www.putnam.com
T. Rowe Price	P.O. Box 17630 Baltimore, MD 21297		www.troweprice.com
Vanguard Group	P.O. Box 1110 Valley Forge, PA 19482	(877) 662-7447	www.vanguard.com

If you're setting up a portfolio that will contain multiple investments, focus on the asset allocation you want and make sure you're comfortable with the approach, level of risk, and types of investments you'll be making.

Based on your goals, intended investment strategy, and time horizon, you should be able to document your asset allocation plans and complete the following worksheet.

Investment Worksheet

Total amount of money to initially invest: $_____

Source(s) of funds to be invested (where the money is now):

❏ Current Paycheck(s) $_____

❏ Bank Checking Account(s) $_____

❏ Bank Savings Account(s) $_____

❏ Money Market Account(s) $_____

❏ Other Current Investment(s) $_____

❏ Other (_____) $_____

❏ Monthly amount to be invested through automatic investing: $_____

Account from which money will be withdrawn: _____

Investment Time Horizon

❏ Less than 2 years

❏ 3 to 5 years

❏ 6 to 10 years

❏ 11 to 20 years

❏ 21 to 30 years

❏ More than 30 years

Intended Investment Strategy

❏ Growth

❏ Income

❏ Growth and Income

Investment Objective and Desired Risk (described in Chapter 4)

❏ Short-Term (Least Risky)
❏ Conservative
❏ Balanced
❏ Growth
❏ Aggressive Growth
❏ Most Aggressive (Riskiest)

Target Portfolio Asset Allocation

Short-Term Investments:	____ %
Stocks and/or Stock Funds:	____ %
Bonds and/or Bond Funds:	____ %
International Investments/Funds:	____ %
Total:	100%

How to Establish Your Account

The first step in establishing an account is to obtain the appropriate account application form from the mutual fund company. If you obtained a printed copy of a prospectus, the form was probably included. You can also complete application forms online, by visiting the mutual fund company's Web site and clicking on "Open an Account."

Investing Tip

ACCOUNT APPLICATIONS Completing an account application will take 15 to 30 minutes, assuming you have at hand all of the information you'll need. The information requested and the order in which it's requested will vary slightly from company to company.

If you're completing a paper application, use a pen with black ink. Also, write legibly!

You'll be asked for the following information:

- Your full name, including middle name or middle initial
- Your Social Security number (or tax identification number)
- Your date of birth
- An acknowledgment that you're a U.S. citizen or U.S. resident alien
- Your driver's license number (possibly)

Investing Tip

JOINT ACCOUNTS If you're creating a *joint account*, you'll need to supply the same information for the account's co-owner. Unless otherwise specified, the co-owner of the account will automatically be registered as a *joint tenant with rights of survivorship*. If you're setting up an individual account, you will be asked to name a beneficiary for that account and provide contact information.

The next section of the account application will typically ask for your contact information. (Again, if you're setting up a joint account, this information will need to be supplied for each account owner.) Requested information will include:

- Your complete street address (no P.O. box)
- Your mailing address, if different from your street address (P.O. box OK)

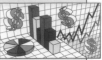

JOINT ACCOUNT An account opened by two people, who then share ownership of the account and its holdings in one of two ways.

Mutual Fund Key Term

JOINT TENANTS WITH RIGHTS OF SURVIVORSHIP Ownership by two or more people where there is no division of the asset. If one owner dies, total ownership passes to the surviving owner(s).

JOINT TENANTS IN COMMON Ownership by two or more people where a percentage of ownership is specified for each owner. If one owner dies, his or her share of the asset passes to his or her estate.

- Your daytime telephone number
- Your evening telephone number
- Your e-mail address

You may also be required to supply alternative contact information, which can be for a spouse, a relative, or a friend who lives at a different address. Some applications also ask you to list your employer, job title, and work address and phone number.

If you're completing the application online, information from your credit report will be accessed automatically. For identification verification purposes only (and to help prevent identity theft), you may be asked specific information about your creditors/lenders. You may also be asked additional information about your investing objectives.

The next step involves listing the mutual fund(s) you wish to invest in and the amount of your initial investment. Remember: to set up a new account or invest in a new fund, you must at least meet the fund's initial investment minimum, which varies by fund and company but is typically $2,500 for non-retirement investments. Within this portion of the account application, you may be asked for a fund code, which you'll find within the fund's prospectus or marketing materials. In addition to providing the appropriate code, be sure to give the fund's complete name.

Using the same application, you can start investing in any number of funds with that company. If you're applying on paper and you want more than two or three funds, you may have to complete your list on a separate sheet of paper, to submit with your application. By law, you're allowed to invest in a fund only *after* the company has provided you with a prospectus, which you can obtain in person, by mail, or online.

After completing the section of the application where you select your investments and determine your initial investment amount, the next portion of the application will allow you to set up automatic investment. As you already know, this option allows the company to deduct an amount that you specify from your checking account every month and invest in the fund(s) you choose.

Setting up automatic investment is totally optional. If you choose to set this up, however, you'll be asked for a start date. Most mutual fund companies use the 15th day of the month for automatic investments; however, you can select the day as well as the start month and year. Next, you'll be asked for the fund code(s) and fund name(s) for the automatic investment and the amount of your monthly investment. All mutual funds have minimum subsequent investment requirements, which can be anywhere from $50 to $250.

Investing Tip

AUTOMATIC DEDUCTIONS Instead of having funds automatically deducted from your checking account, you can often instruct the mutual fund company to automatically deduct the funds directly from your paycheck, especially if you're investing into a retirement account.

The next decision you'll need to make as you complete the account application is whether or not you want your dividend distributions and capital gains distributions automatically reinvested or sent to your home address. You'll need to specify your decisions about dividend distributions and capital gains distributions separately, since you can have them treated differently or the same. If you want maximum income from your investments, you can have all distributions sent to you by check. If your goal is to build wealth and increase your portfolio, you can reinvest all distributions. In some cases, you can choose to have income generated from one mutual fund invested in another mutual fund.

Before you complete the account application, there will be a reminder to review all fees associated with each fund. Some mutual fund companies will allow you to receive full-service, writing-only support and service or online-only service. Your choice will help determine your account fees. Full service means you have access to customer service representatives by telephone, by mail, or online and can conduct many transactions in person, online, by mail, or by telephone. If you opt for the writing-only option, you must conduct all business in writing. Likewise, if you choose the online account management option, you must use the company's Web site for all business pertaining to your funds.

Regardless of the option you choose, you'll then have to indicate how you want to receive your investor documents, such as your shareholder reports or annual reports. You can choose to receive these documents (and other materials from the company) at your home address (by mail) or to receive these documents via e-mail.

The final section of most account applications requires you to sign and date the application. If you have a power of attorney, this person will need to sign and date the application as well. Near your signature, you'll also be required to print your full name. If your application is online, you cannot physically sign it, of course. Instead, legal information will be displayed. You must click on the "Agree" icon to continue.

Investing Tip

DEDUCTIONS FOR CHECKING If you're having funds deducted from your checking account, you will be required to submit a voided check with your application. (Write the word "Void" in large letters across the front of a blank check. Make sure you don't cover the routing number and checking account number at the bottom of the check.)

If your application is paper, you must then mail it to the address listed on the application, with a check or money order for your initial investment and any other required documentation specified on the application. Before mailing the application and any materials, photocopy everything. Then, send the package, using an overnight courier (such as FedEx, UPS, or DHL) that can be tracked or take advantage of the U.S. Postal Service's "Delivery Confirmation" service. If using an overnight courier, you'll need to provide a mailing address for the mutual fund company that is not a P.O. box.

Investing Tip

WHAT TO REMEMBER Once your account is set up, be sure to write down your account number and all of the information you'll need to access your account online, including your username or user ID and your password. You'll want to keep this information confidential.

When it's time to transfer money to fund your account, you can provide the mutual fund company with a check or money order or complete additional forms allowing for funds to be wired to your new account, transferred from your checking or savings account, or transferred from another existing investment account. If you'll be having funds transferred from your checking account, for example, you'll need to provide the name of your bank, its address, its routing number, and your account number.

After the company receives your application and the necessary funds, the time to open the account and to purchase

Mutual Funds: A Quick-Start Guide

Investing Tip

If you're investing for the first time, consider opening your account in person by visiting a customer service office operated by the mutual fund company. Another alternative is to call the company's toll-free number and ask to speak with a specialist who can walk you through the process and answer any questions as you proceed. Before committing your money, make sure you understand the investing process, all risks and fees, and the type of investments you're making.

your initial shares will be anywhere from one to five business days, depending on the company. The price you pay for each fund share will be the NAV calculated on the end of the day on which the mutual fund company processes your transactions and establishes the account. After any fees are deducted, the company will provide you with a statement listing your initial holdings: the fund(s) you own, the number of shares you've purchased, the purchase date, the purchase price per share, and any fees deducted.

By opening an account and buying your first mutual fund(s), you will have established an investment portfolio. You can add to your portfolio at any time by making additional investments in the fund(s) you own, purchasing shares of new funds, or adding other types of investments to your portfolio (such as individual stocks or bonds), if your mutual fund company also offers a brokerage service, which is almost always the case.

Investing Tip

MONEY HELD BY BROKER Money that the mutual fund company or broker holds before putting it into funds will typically be held in a money market account.

Taking Care of Your Portfolio

Now that you have a portfolio, you need to manage it properly so that you adhere to your investment strategies and objectives. Chapter 7 focuses on how to manage your portfolio. You can do this easily using a portfolio management program, either online or on your computer.

Investing Tip

PURPOSEFUL PORTFOLIOS Many investors set up different portfolios for different purposes. For example, they'll have one for their retirement, one for their child's college education, and one for wealth building. The goals and time horizon are different for each portfolio, requiring different asset allocation and investment strategies. Most mutual fund companies will help you set up and manage multiple portfolios with a single account, which makes it easier to keep records for tax purposes, etc.

Purchase a file cabinet or storage box where you can store all of the materials associated with your investments safely and in an organized manner. Keep a written record of your portfolio, starting immediately by listing the fund(s) you own, the number of shares you've purchased, and the purchase price of those shares. You'll also want to keep a record of expenses and fees paid and the dates of all transactions. The following worksheet will help you keep track of this information.

Investment Portfolio Worksheet   Date: ___/___/___

Mutual Fund Name	Symbol	Purchase Price per Share ($)	Transaction Date	Number of Shares	Fees ($)	Total ($)
					Total Portfolio Value	$

Later, as you're managing your portfolio, you can easily calculate its total value by obtaining current quotes for the funds you own and doing some basic math. How to obtain quotes and keep tabs on your investments is covered within Chapter 7. You can also keep tabs on how your investments are performing and whether you're losing money on any of them. This is all part of what's involved with managing your portfolio.

You'll soon learn that many of the Web sites operated by the mutual fund companies offer free, online-based *portfolio management tools*. Similar tools are also offered (free of charge) by independent personal finance Web sites. If you're an AOL member, for example, simply click on the "Finance" icon and select "Investing" from the pull-down menu to access power-ful, online portfolio management tools. Chapter 7 offers more information about other online and software portfolio man-agement tools that make it extremely easy to keep tabs on your mutual fund portfolio and to conduct analysis and research.

PORTFOLIO MANAGEMENT TOOL An online or soft-ware application for tracking investments.

Mutual Fund Key Term

Investing Tip

SOFTWARE TO HELP Fund Manager (*www.fundmanagersoftware.com*), a software package developed by Beiley Software, Inc., is an example of a portfolio management tool designed specifically for mutual fund investors. The personal version of this software is priced at $69.00.

If you're investing for a long term, it will probably be ade-quate to check on your investments every three to six months. If you're investing for the short term and/or in high-risk investments, you'll want to keep closer tabs on your portfolio. Some of the questions you should ask yourself about your portfolio's performance and adjusting your holdings periodi-cally will be covered in the next chapter.

Managing Your Portfolio

WHAT'S IN THIS CHAPTER

- How to manage your portfolio properly
- Gathering and entering all pertinent information
- What managing a mutual fund portfolio entails
- Portfolio management tools you can use
- Keeping on target to achieve your goals
- An interview with a mutual fund investment advisor

By now, you should understand the basic steps involved in investing in mutual funds, which will be recapped in this chapter. For some or all of these steps, you may opt to work with a financial planner or investment advisor. No matter how you choose to proceed, it's essential that you understand how mutual fund investments work, know what you're investing in, and establish realistic expectations for your portfolio's performance.

This chapter focuses primarily on the last step—managing your portfolio and performing periodic checkups to ensure that its overall performance is in line with your goals. There are many reasons to manage your portfolio properly, including the following:

- So you always know what investments you own and the value of your portfolio
- So you can file your tax returns correctly and easily
- So you can ensure that your investments are meeting your expectations and that your portfolio's performance and asset allocation are on target to achieve your goals within your time horizon
- So you can keep tabs on the fees and charges you're paying
- So you can alter your investing strategy as you reach milestones

The Ten Basic Steps to Mutual Fund Investing

Everything you've read thus far in this book can be summed up in ten basic steps to smart investing in mutual funds. Of course, you could skip one or two of these steps, but then you would increase the chances that you *won't* achieve your investment goals. You'll most likely wind up with a hodge-podge of investments for which you're paying fees but from which you're not getting the returns you want.

For example, if you fail to set realistic goals before you start investing, you begin the investing process with no target and no direction. This makes it virtually impossible to choose the right mix of investments for your portfolio. Likewise, if you skip setting a time horizon, you won't be able to choose specific investments efficiently, as different categories of mutual funds will generate very different results over time. Each step you skip in the process will have a different nega- tive impact on the performance of your portfolio and the returns it generates. Thus, it's smart to follow each of the ten key steps:

1. Set your investment goals.
2. Establish a time horizon.
3. Choose a level of risk tolerance.
4. Calculate how much money you'll invest initially and how much you'll invest every month through an auto- matic investment plan.
5. Determine a target for your portfolio asset allocation.

6. Select a mutual fund company that's well-established and reputable and that offers the services you want and need at a reasonable cost.
7. Create and fund an account.
8. Research specific mutual funds that are appropriate for your portfolio and goals, read the prospectus and share-holder agreement for each fund, and obtain third-party research.
9. Buy shares of mutual funds to establish your portfolio.
10. Manage your portfolio and perform checkups periodically (every six to 12 months).

How to Manage Your Portfolio Properly

One of the best things about managing a mutual fund portfolio is that it's typically very easy. If you invested in individual stocks or other types of investments, you'd most likely need to carefully watch each investment daily or at least weekly, especially if those investments were riskier small- or mid-cap stocks or other highly volatile holdings.

Your mutual fund investments, however, are being managed by professionals. Thus, your primary responsibility in managing your portfolio is basically to keep tabs on overall performance and to ensure that the investments in your portfolio are working together toward achieving your goals. This requires that you check your portfolio every six to 12 months—not daily, weekly, or even monthly.

You'll want to use an online or software portfolio management tool. This dramatically reduces the time required to properly manage your portfolio, because much of the work you need to do, such as keeping track of your portfolio's current value, becomes totally automated.

To start managing your portfolio, first gather up all of the pertinent information that you need to track (see the next section) and then choose a portfolio management tool with the functions you want and need. These tools are available, free of charge, from most mutual fund company Web sites and from many investment-oriented Web sites. Popular online services like AOL (*finance.aol.com/usw/portfolios/myportfolios*) also offer easy-to-use, online portfolio managers to members.

For under $100, you can also purchase a software portfolio management tool or a more comprehensive personal financial management tool, like Quicken or Microsoft Money Deluxe, both of which include a portfolio manager module. Later in this chapter you'll read more about some of the many online and software portfolio management tools.

Gather and Enter All Pertinent Information

To properly manage your portfolio, you must start with accurate information. Using the statements provided by your mutual fund company, start by making a detailed list of every mutual fund and other type of investment you own. For each mutual fund, you'll need to gather the following information:

- Name
- Ticker symbol

- Number of shares initially purchased
- Purchase price per share
- Date of the initial purchase
- Fees (commissions or loads) paid for the shares purchased

You'll need the same information for any additional investments you make, whether through an automatic investment plan or otherwise.

You enter this information into your portfolio management program, which keeps all of this information in a database. Then, the program will use information and data from the Internet (free of charge in most cases) to keep the financial information for your portfolio up-to-date.

Warning

BE ACCURATE When manually entering information about your holdings into a portfolio manager, it's essential to enter it accurately. You can always update or correct information, but the calculations, reports, summaries, and analyses prepared by the mutual fund management tool will be based on the information you enter.

A basic portfolio management tool will allow you to do the following:

- View details about your investments and the current value of each investment and the current value of your portfolio
- View the gain or loss of each investment and the overall gain or loss of your portfolio

- Chart or graph the portfolio of any investment or of your portfolio
- Calculate taxable income from your investments that you must report to the IRS
- Access current news headlines pertaining to your individual investments
- Perform analyses of your investments and your portfolio, relating to performance, risk, asset allocation, and/or diversification

Some portfolio management tools offer considerably more functions, allowing investors to analyze individual investments, review asset allocation, and look at a portfolio's current positioning and historic performance (by including details about purchases, sales, and other transactions).

Using almost any portfolio management tool, you can easily keep track of all your investments, even if you've invested with more than one mutual fund company and also own shares of individual stocks, for example.

Investing Tip

FREE STUFF The portfolio management tools offered free of charge typically have fewer functions than commercial tools, but are adequate for many novice investors. If you want to be able to access analysis, create details charts and graphics, and obtain financial data beyond a fund's current NAV and performance history, you might opt to pay for a portfolio management tool with the added functions you need.

The Portfolio Management Tool Offered by Your Mutual Fund Company

All of the popular mutual fund companies offer their investors, free of charge, a similar online portfolio management tool with access to the Internet. In many cases, data from your account will automatically be incorporated into the portfolio management tool, so you do not need to do any manual data entry or financial calculations at all.

If you're an investor with Fidelity Investments, for example, you'll automatically receive access to its online portfolio management tool, with a robust collection of functions. For example, with a click of the mouse, you can instantly view a summary of your portfolio and your portfolio positions (details about current value and changes to value), access portfolio research (information about your investments and performance charts and graphs), obtain a portfolio analysis (including a pie chart showing your asset allocation, an equity style profile, and an equity industry sector chart), and access to your Fidelity printed statements (as well as tax forms, the most current shareholder reports, the prospectus for each fund you own, and a summary of all investment transactions).

The Portfolio Management Tool Offered by Morningstar

The online portfolio manager offered by Morningstar takes just minutes to set up, but offers a lot of functions. After you've entered the pertinent portfolio information once, anytime you use this tool you'll view a Morningstar Portfolio Manager Snapshot chart containing the information displayed below.

Morningstar Portfolio Manager (Snapshot)

Name	Current Price ($)	Price Change ($)	Price Change (%)	Shares Held	Market Value ($)	Weight (%)	News	Analysis Report [Date]	Morningstar Rating for Fund	Morningstar Rating for Stocks
				YOUR INFORMATION HERE						

Above this table on your computer screen will be menu icons that you can click to use online tools to analyze your individual fund investments and your portfolio. For example, click on the "Performance" icon to see a colorful chart and summary of your portfolio's performance over the past 12 weeks, 12 months, or 12 quarters. Click on the "Gain/Loss" icon to see how each fund in your portfolio has performed and determine your gain or loss since the date of purchase, displayed as a dollar value and as a percentage, as well as the total year-to-date return for each fund and for your portfolio. Click on the "Fundamental" icon to obtain details about each fund's category, see a Morningstar Style Box for that fund, and view additional analytical information provided by Morningstar. Below this table on your computer screen will be a list of news headlines pertaining to each mutual fund you own.

You can also opt for a Snapshot View Print Report of your portfolio, which will be a table like the one below with all of your portfolio's current financial data. In other words, you'll never have to perform any mathematical calculations or analysis by hand in order to acquire basic information about your portfolio.

Re-Creation of Morningstar's Snapshot View Print Report

Portfolio Name _____

Current Date _____

Current Value of the Portfolio: $_____

Holding Name	Ticker	Security Type	Shares	Current Price	Price Change (%)	Change in Value ($)	Market Value ($)	% of Portfolio Weight
		YOUR INFORMATION HERE						
Total								%

Investing Tip

MORNINGSTAR BENEFITS If you subscribe to Morningstar's premium service, you can also instantly obtain a Portfolio Overview X-Ray Report and more detailed analysis from Morningstar. You'll also have access to the company's proprietary Asset Allocator, Portfolio Allocator, and Risk Analyzer tools.

Warning

INPUT THE DATA ACCURATELY While the analysis and research functions of a mutual fund manager tool created by a third party, such as Morningstar, will probably be more robust than what your mutual fund company offers, you may have to input your financial data manually—and accurately—when you initially set up the portfolio management tool.

Additional Portfolio Management Tools You Can Use

In addition to the portfolio management tools offered by mutual fund companies and Morningstar, you'll find similar tools available at various popular personal finance and investment-related Web sites (many of which are described in Appendix A).

The following is information about a few additional online and software portfolio management tools you can use for your mutual fund investments:

ES Quotes—This program from Gilmore Software Development (*www.esquotes.com*, $29.00) is a powerful Microsoft Excel workbook with a Dynamic Link Library that allows investors to manage their portfolios using a pre-created Microsoft Excel spreadsheet. Once loaded, the spreadsheet automatically downloads current quotes from the Internet and performs performance calculations on each holding and on the portfolio. A trial version of ES Quotes can be downloaded from the company's Web site. You must have Microsoft Excel installed on your computer to use this application.

Fund Manager—This program from Beiley Software (*www.fundmanagersoftware.com*, $69.00 for the personal version) offers an abundance of powerful tools suitable for intermediate and expert investors, although without bells and whistles to make it look pretty on your computer screen. The software allows users to print 13 types of reports and create 29 types of graphs.

Because the software automatically retrieves current quotes from the Internet, it allows investors to keep constant tabs on their portfolios and individual investments. An investor's portfolio information can also automatically be imported from company Web sites such as TD Ameritrade and TD Waterhouse, Fidelity, and SchwabLink.

FundBuilder Software—This software from FundBuilder Technology (*www.fundbuilder.com*) contains several investment planning calculators and taps the power of the Internet to provide a nice selection of portfolio management tools and analysis. You can download a free trial version of this software from the company's Web site.

Microsoft Money Deluxe—This is a full-featured, easy-to-use, highly graphic personal finance management tool designed to help users manage all aspects of their finances, not just investments. What's nice about this type of comprehensive personal finance package is that details about your investment portfolio can seamlessly be incorporated into your budget, online banking, and accounting records. This package is available wherever Microsoft software is sold and it can be downloaded from the company Web site (*www.microsoft.com*, $49.99).

MSN Money Investment Toolbox—This is a handful of investment tools available from the MSN Money Web site (*moneycentral.msn.com/investor/controls/setup.asp*), including a feature-packed portfolio management application that's easy to use. To use these tools, you'll need to download free, specialized software that works in conjunction with the MSN Money Web site.

Quicken Premiere—Developed by Intuit Software, Quicken is one of the most popular personal finance software packages available to computer users. It's designed to easily help users manage all aspects of their personal finances, including online banking, budgeting, spending, and investing. Like Microsoft Money, the portfolio management module of this software seamlessly integrates with the rest of the software. This is particularly useful for overall budgeting and tax reporting. One nice feature of the portfolio management module is that you can instantly compare your portfolio's performance with market averages. The software can be purchased on CD-ROM from software retailers nationwide or downloaded from Intuit's Web site (*www.quicken.com*), which also offers a variety of free investment tools and other resources.

Warning

MORE INFORMATION The interview with Quicken's senior product manager, John Flora, in this chapter gives more information about how investors use this popular software.

SmartMoney.com's Portfolio Manager and Portfolio Map—The online portfolio manager is both easy to use and powerful. One interesting feature it offers is the Portfolio Map. This tool organizes your portfolio into a color-coded graphic display, enabling you to track performance based on information that appears in a series of colorful, on-screen rectangles that represent your mutual funds and/or stocks. The size of each rectangle corresponds to the relative value of that investment in your portfolio and the color indicates performance (green if the price is up and red if the price is down).

Investing Tip

USING YOUR PHONE With a Palm OS Smartphone, you can use portfolio management software from virtually anywhere. To find a Palm OS portfolio management tool with the functions you want and need, visit the Palm Software online store (*www.palm.com/us/software/index.html*) and do a search for a "portfolio manager." One option is the Money Magazine Financial Assistant package from LandWare, Inc. (*www.landware.com* $19.95). This company also offers a Palm OS version of Quicken, Pocket Quicken.

Advice from an Expert: John Flora, Senior Product Manager for Quicken

Quicken from Intuit Software is one of the world's leading personal finance software packages. This PC- and Mac-based software package has been around for 23 years and is used by more than 15 million people. You can obtain more information about this software and use a wide range of online personal finance tools at the company's Web site, *www.quicken.com*. The Basic version is priced at $29.99, with a Deluxe at $49.99, a Premier at $69.99, and a Home & Business at $79.99, with the most comprehensive set of tools for investors. With each new (annual) edition, Quicken gets upgraded with additional features and feature enhancements. The focus in recent years has been to provide a comprehensive personal finance solution that's extremely easy to use and that requires only minutes to customize and set up with your personal financial data.

One of the useful tools for mutual fund investors in this software package is the Portfolio Manager, which allows you to automatically upload account-specific information and financial data directly from your mutual fund company. The software also offers many of the same powerful investment, research, and analysis tools you'll find in other portfolio management applications.

As the senior product manager for Quicken at Intuit Software, John Flora is responsible for ensuring that the software is powerful, offers the features users want and need, and remains easy to use even for people who aren't financially savvy. In this interview, he explains some of the ways investors benefit from using Quicken as their primary personal finance management tool.

What exactly is Quicken and how can it be used?

John Flora: "Quicken is a personal finance management tool that offers a single place to review and organize personal finance information and perform all of the finance-related tasks users need to do, including online banking. Our typical user is someone who is concerned about better controlling their spending and saving, because they are managing their family's finances. We also see a lot of people using this software to manage their finances after retirement."

What would you say is the most compelling reason to use Quicken?

John Flora: "Quicken can download all of your financial information, relating to all of your financial relationships, whether it's your checking account information from your bank, or your mutual fund investments from the company you invest with. Quicken gathers this information and puts it all in one place automatically. You're then able to do really deep analysis about your spending, savings, tax liabilities, and investing. The software offers a traditional portfolio management feature, plus additional tools for managing all of your investments."

What are some of the tools within the portfolio manager?

John Flora: "A user can evaluate individual stocks and mutual funds, access Morningstar ratings, and gather news headlines pertaining to investments. Quicken also offers an asset allocation tool and a risk profile tool. Using these tools, Quicken is able to help you determine if you're investing in a way that will help you reach the targets you've set for yourself. The basic portfolio manager is available in all versions of Quicken. The Quicken Deluxe package offers a handful of additional tools for managing retirement accounts. Quicken Premier offers all this, plus additional investment analysis tools."

How long does it take the typical user to set up Quicken and start using it?

John Flora: "If you're an online banking customer with any traditional bank, you can set up and start using Quicken in under 15 minutes. All of your personal financial data and account information will be downloaded and incorporated into the software automatically."

Do you have any specific tips on how a mutual fund investor can best use Quicken?

John Flora: "For novice investors in particular, mutual funds are used as a way to save money. Our software focuses on helping people save money, manage their budget, control spending, and develop a complete understanding of their current financial situation. Quicken can help you manage an automatic investment plan with any mutual fund company, for example. It can be used as a tool for monitoring your savings and investments.

"Quicken makes it easier to establish better financial habits, whether it has to do with spending, saving, or investing. Using our software, you'll probably be able to find more money in your budget to invest, and then be able to use Quicken to help those investments grow faster over time."

What Managing a Mutual Fund Portfolio Entails

Most mutual fund investment experts (including those interviewed throughout this book) recommend that an investor spend the time necessary to create a well-balanced and diversified mutual fund portfolio to achieve a specific goal within a specific time horizon. Once the portfolio is established, these experts recommend checking on its performance once or twice per year—not every day, every week, or even every month, which is a potentially bad habit that many first-time investors acquire.

Mutual fund investments are designed to generate returns over the long term. So, once you establish your portfolio and set up a portfolio manager tool to help you track your investments, use this tool once every few months to ensure that your investment strategy is working and that your portfolio is properly diversified. If you check your portfolio every six months and notice dramatic losses with a particular investment or your investment goals change, you might then consider making adjustments to your holdings, as needed.

When you perform a semiannual or annual checkup of your portfolio, this is the time to look at your portfolio's total return and at the dividend and capital gains distributions made by each of your funds. Also, look at share price changes and determine if the overall performance of your funds is meeting or exceeding your expectations. All of the mathematical calculations you'll need to obtain this information will probably be done automatically by the portfolio manager tool you use.

As you examine your portfolio's performance, compare each investment against a specific benchmark, such as the S&P 500. This will help you determine if you could improve overall performance by changing some of your investments or reworking your asset allocation. Even in a bear market, if your portfolio is properly diversified, you should keep your losses under control. Remember: if you're not happy with how your portfolio is performing or it's performing worse than key benchmarks, you can contact an investment advisor for assistance in getting your portfolio on track.

BEAR MARKET A market in which the values of securities or commodities are persistently declining.

BULL MARKET A market in which the values of securities or commodities are persistently rising.

Mutual Fund Key Term

When evaluating your portfolio, ask yourself these questions:

- Are your investments generating better returns than you'd earn if your money were in a basic savings account, a money market account, or certificates of deposit?
- Has each of your investments performed better than other similar funds in the same category?
- How is your portfolio performing against a benchmark, such as the S&P 500?
- Is your portfolio on track to meet or exceed your performance expectations and achieve your long-term financial goals?

- Are there any areas where your portfolio is lacking? Could it be better diversified? Should the asset allocation of your portfolio be adjusted to better align with your goals?

Before making any drastic changes to your portfolio, examine how each of your funds is performing. If, for example, one fund hasn't performed well over the past year, do some research to determine how similar funds have performed during the same period. Only if you notice that your fund is having problems that similar funds in the same category are not should you consider making some changes to your holdings. Even if this is the case, don't act rashly!

Warning

KEEP YOUR PORTFOLIO STABLE Don't make drastic changes to your investment mix too often. Once you've developed a portfolio that you're comfortable with, adjustments to that mutual fund portfolio should not be necessary more than once every five or so years. If you do a good job selecting a diversified selection of mutual funds initially, they should serve you well over the long term with little adjustment. Even if the performance of your funds falters temporarily, don't panic, especially if your time horizon is ten, 15, 20, or 30 years.

Investing Tip

TAX TIME As you prepare your annual tax returns, you'll want to check your portfolio so you can accurately document capital gains and dividend distributions you've received and that have to be reported to the IRS.

Advice from an Expert: Michael McLaughlin, CFP and ChFC

Michael McLaughlin is a CFP and a ChFC (Chartered Financial Consultant) who is a principal in Vanguard's Advice Services Group. He has been with the company for 15 years and currently spends much of his time helping Vanguard's investors choose the right mutual funds and then manage their portfolios by providing them with expert advice and guidance. He also oversees a team of about 100 financial planners. In this interview, he shares some of his best advice.

Based in Valley Force, Pennsylvania, The Vanguard Group was founded in May 1975. As of December 2005, the company managed a total of $950 billion in its mutual funds, which include 130 domestic funds and 40 funds in international markets. The company manages over 21.5 million institutional and individual shareholder accounts and in the United States employs over 11,500 people.

In addition to its brokerage and other investment services, Vanguard manages a wide range of highly rated mutual funds in every category. This allows you to mix money market

Investing Tip

ONE-STOP SHOPS Like Fidelity Investments and T. Rowe Price, for example, Vanguard is a one-stop shop for all of your investing needs. For more information about Vanguard and its mutual funds and services, call (877) 662-7447 or visit *www.vanguard.com*. For information about Vanguard's retirement planning services, call (800) 414-1321.

funds, bond funds, stock funds, and balanced ("life cycle") funds to create a portfolio to meet your goals. The most famous mutual funds operated by Vanguard are the Vanguard Wellington Fund (founded in 1929 by the Wellington Management Company as the Industrial and Power Securities Co.) and the Vanguard 500 Index Fund (founded in 1976 and now the world's largest mutual fund).

According to the company, "Vanguard's mission is to help clients reach their financial goals by being the world's highest-value provider of investment products and services."

As a CFP in Vanguard's Advice Services Group, what are your primary responsibilities?

Michael McLaughlin: "We provide investors with advice about asset allocation and portfolio construction. We also help people determine if they're saving and investing enough to achieve their long-term financial goals. Many of our clients are self-directed investors who manage their own portfolios, but who want a second option from us, in terms of their investment strategies. People come to Vanguard because of the services we offer and our long-term reputation for controlling costs. All of our planners are salaried employees. We don't receive a bonus or commission based on any of the advice we offer.

"I am a firm believer in seeking out a second opinion. This is the advice I offer to all mutual fund investors, even if they want to make their own investing decisions. Talking

---

to a professional about your investment approach and strategies is always a good idea. We have expertise helping people plan for major life events. We can help you determine where you are and what you need to do in order to achieve your goals."

What types of tools does Vanguard offer to investors?

Michael McLaughlin: "We offer a full spectrum of investment tools through our Web site, as well as tutorials and educational information. We also offer the one-on-one advice from our financial experts. On the Web site [*www.Vanguard.com*], you'll find a fund selector and asset allocation tool to help you choose the best funds and properly diversify your portfolio. You'll also find an investment questionnaire on the Web site to help you set your investment goals, determine your comfort level with risk, and choose the most optimal investment strategies based on your goals and time horizon.

"Our advice and tools are designed to help investors start by selecting the most suitable asset allocation to meet their needs. This means figuring out how much of your mutual fund portfolio you want to have in stocks, bonds, and cash. You can then look at how each of these categories has performed in the past to determine risk level and whether the asset allocation you set as your target is realistic for achieving your objectives."

What are some of the biggest mistakes you see mutual fund investors make?

Michael McLaughlin: "People tend to overanalyze their holdings and their portfolio as a whole. There is so much information and data out there, investors think they have to utilize every piece of it that's available in order to be successful. Also, clients often overreact to the current environment and don't put it into the proper context. People try to overanalyze patterns. No matter what you invest in, over time there are going to be short-term positive and negative spurts. Another problem is that once mutual fund investors set up their portfolio, they have trouble sitting back and doing nothing. They feel like they should be constantly doing something to manage that portfolio, even when there is nothing whatsoever they should be doing.

"The goal of every mutual fund investor should be to meet their goals and objectives. You need to ask yourself if each investment vehicle will allow you to do this, while allowing you to reduce the risk and volatility associated with your returns. Sure, an individual stock might allow you to hit a home run with high returns, but you're taking on significant risk.

"Another common mistake is that some people own shares of 20 or even 30 different mutual funds, but have absolutely no clue what they actually own, in terms of the holdings of each of those funds. More often than not, the funds they own have a tremendous and unnecessary overlap in holdings. People are overdiversified.

"People are also tempted to chase performance. They look at sectors or industries that are experiencing very strong short-term performance and lose sight of their long-term goals. In many cases, that short-term performance people see in a specific sector or industry is not sustainable."

What tips can you share for managing a mutual fund portfolio?

Michael McLaughlin: "If you feel comfortable with the way your portfolio's asset allocation is set and you have a well-diversified portfolio, at most you should only look at your portfolio twice each year. The only time you need to review your portfolio more often is if your goals, time horizon, or risk tolerance dramatically changes. If, however, you have an asset allocation formula you're comfortable with, the most you should need to do is make minor changes to readjust your portfolio once or twice per year, to make sure it follows that formula. Don't overreact even if one or two funds are underperforming compared to a benchmark for a short time, when your time horizon is 15, 20, or 30 years. If that fund is underperforming year after year, for three or more years in a row, that's when you might want to make adjustments.

"When reviewing your portfolio, make sure each fund is staying true to its investment objective and mandate. If there has been a major change with the fund's strategy or the fund's manager and that fund isn't performing well over a period of two or three years, consider getting into another similar fund. When investing in mutual funds over a long period, don't concern yourself with short-term fluctuations."

What are some of the most common questions you receive from clients?

Michael McLaughlin: "People always ask about the returns they can expect from their mutual fund investments. I find that a lot of people have a strong misconception about what to expect. If someone says they're expecting an annual return of 18 to 20 percent per year, that's a red flag and unrealistic. People often ask why a portion of their portfolio should incorporate bond funds. As a bond fund investor, you should be looking at their long-term income stream and use these funds to counterbalance the risk and volatility of the stock funds in your portfolio.

"Another common question is whether someone should invest in international funds. Again, this is a way to diversify a portfolio. If someone has 50 percent of their holdings in equity [stock] funds, we might recommend that 10 to 20 percent of that be in international funds, based the risk tolerance, desired goals, and the time horizon. International funds perform differently than domestic stock funds."

In terms of international funds, what do you recommend?

Michael McLaughlin: "If someone were to allocate 30 percent of their total mutual fund portfolio to international funds, I might recommend going with 80 percent of that into developed countries and 20 percent into emerging market funds. This is a somewhat conservative, but effective approach."

Is there any other investing advice you can share?

Michael McLaughlin: "Don't allow the current environment to blind you to your long-term goals. Short-term focus can really screw up investors. It's tempting to jump into a certain marketplace when it's going well, without considering what will happen if there's a sudden downturn in that sector of the market, whether it's high-tech, dotcoms, energy, or real estate, for example."

Final Thoughts

Becoming an investor can be stressful, especially if you're not accustomed to dealing with the risks of investing and you don't like seeing fluctuations in your portfolio's value. Remember: investing in mutual funds is not a get-rich-quick scheme. Investing in a well-diversified mutual fund portfolio will most likely allow you to generate favorable results over the long term and help you save for major life events, such as buying a big-ticket item, paying for college, or preparing for your retirement.

This book was written to help you understand the pros and cons of mutual fund investing and provide you with the core knowledge you need to get started. Depending on your comfort level, now is the time to consider seeking the help of an investment advisor. You'll find knowledgeable and experienced advisors by contacting any of the major mutual fund companies (Fidelity, Charles Schwab, T. Rowe Price, Vanguard, etc.). As you know, you can also hire an independent advisor to ensure that you're receiving totally unbiased advice.

If you're willing to invest some time to learn how to perform research and analysis yourself or at least to understand the information you acquire from a reputable source, such as Morningstar, you'll probably have little trouble establishing and managing your mutual fund investment portfolio with little or no outside help. (If you're investing for retirement, however, definitely consider working with a specialist who will help you profit from all of the tax benefits associated with this type of investing.)

To learn more about mutual funds and to obtain timely and useful information about specific funds, use the Recommended Reading list in Appendix A. Also, take full advantage of the many online tools and resources described throughout this book.

As long as you can gather enough money to meet the minimum initial investment requirements of a mutual fund company, there's no better time than right now to get started. In fact, a few companies offer automatic investment programs for some of their funds that allow you to get started with only a $50 investment (instead of $2,500), as long as you'll commit to making a regular monthly investment of at least $50.

Investing in mutual funds is a wonderful way to save for the future, build a financial nest egg, and achieve your long-term financial objectives. The information in this book has provided you with the foundation of knowledge you'll need to get started. The next step is to take action and start investing in mutual funds.

Recommended Reading

The following is a listing of magazines, newspapers, Web sites, newsletters, and other resources of interest to mutual fund investors. Some of these publications and services are by subscription (fee), while others are offered free of charge.

Barron's (800 975-8620/*www.barrons.com*)—This is a well-respected, weekly financial newspaper published by Dow Jones & Company. It's been around for more than 85 years and is more suitable for serious or experienced investors. (Print edition subscription: $79.00 per year.) The Barron's Web site offers free articles, resources, and online tools for investors.

Charles Schwab (*www.schwab.com*)—The Web site of this full-service broker and mutual fund company offers an informative collection of how-to articles and online tools suitable for investors at all levels. Some of the tools are available only to shareholders or account holders.

CNBC.com (*www.cnbc.com*)—This site, re launched December 4, 2006, by the company after partnering for five years with MSN for MSN Money. It offers financial news and analysis as well as three to eight hours of live programming daily, "covering events that have the potential to move markets" and a live newscast, Market in a Minute, at the top and bottom of each hour between 9:30 A.M. and 4:30 P.M. ET.

CNN Money (*money.cnn.com*)—The Internet home of *Money* and *Fortune* magazines, the CNN Money Web site is intended to be a comprehensive personal finance resource. It contains a vast amount of information about mutual funds. Start your visit to this site by clicking on the "Personal Finance" icon and then the "Funds" icon. The articles, news headlines, and tutorials are divided into several categories, based on investing goals.

Entrepreneur Press (*www.entrepreneurpress.com*)—Learn about other books in *Entrepreneur Magazine's Pocket Guides* series

written by bestselling author Jason R. Rich
(*www.jasonrich.com*).

Fidelity Investments (*www.fidelity.com*)—The Web site of this full-service broker and mutual fund company offers an informative collection of how-to articles and online tools suitable for investors at all levels. Some of the tools are available only to shareholders or account holders, but others are offered free of charge to anyone. For help planning your retirement, visit *www.fidelity.com/plan*.

Franklin Templeton Investments (*www.franklintempleton.com*)— The Web site of this full-service broker and mutual fund company offers how-to articles and online tools suitable for investors at all levels.

Forbes (800 429-0106 / *www.forbes.com*)—This is a biweekly, full-color magazine available from newsstands or by subscription ($19.95 for 26 issues). It's a general-interest personal finance magazine targeted to middle- to high-income business professionals and entrepreneurs.

Fortune (800 621-8000 / *money.cnn.com/magazines/fortune*)— This is a biweekly, full-color magazine available from newsstands or by subscription ($19.99 for 25 issues). It's a general-interest personal finance magazine targeted to middle- to high-income business professionals and entrepreneurs. The online edition of this magazine is part of the

Google Finance (*finance.google.com/finance*)—The popular Google search engine offers a free personal finance Web site that caters to investors. Here you'll find news headlines, articles and quotes.

GreenMoney Journal (*www.greenmoneyjournal.com*)—This is an online version of a quarterly publication for socially and environmentally responsible investors. Here, you can find information about specialty mutual funds.

Investopedia.com (*www.investopedia.com*)—This Web site offers a selection of investing tutorials, how-to articles, and a comprehensive financial dictionary.

Investor's Business Daily (800 831-2525 / *www.investors.com*)—This daily newspaper covers a wide range of topics of interest to all investors. Most of the articles tend to be somewhat technical; however, the newspaper also lists daily information about mutual funds and stock performance. The Web site features a nice selection of online investing tools, plus news headlines and articles.

Kiplinger's Personal Finance (*www.kiplinger.com/personalfinance/magazine*)—This is a monthly, full-color investing and personal finance magazine of interest to all investors. (Subscription rate: $12.00 per year, 12 issues.) The Web site offers a vast amount of information and tools of interest to mutual fund investors.

Marketplace Money Radio Show (*marketplace.publicradio.org*)—Produced by American Public Media, this is a highly entertaining and informative radio program that covers all aspects of personal finance and investing. The weekend edition is one hour long, while the shorter daily edition airs as part of the "Marketplace" program on NPR radio stations nationwide. The program can also be heard anytime online.

MarketWatch (*www.marketwatch.com*)—This is a finance-oriented Web site operated by Dow Jones. Here you'll find an assortment of informative articles, online investing tools, and stock quotes. There's a whole area of this Web site dedicated to mutual fund investing and exchange-traded funds (ETFs). The resources you'll find here are suitable for novice investors. Online tools available include a free fund selector and a top-25 list of mutual funds by fund type, based on returns.

Money (800 633-9970 / *www.money.com*)—This is a monthly, full-color magazine that offers easy-to-understand articles of interest to all investors. It covers a wide range of personal finance-related topics, including retirement and mutual fund investing. The magazine is available from newsstands or by subscription ($9.95 for 13 issues).

Morningstar Publications—In addition to offering one of the most comprehensive set of online tools and resources for mutual fund investors from its Web site (*www.morningstar. com*), Morningstar also publishes newsletters and publications of interest to more serious mutual fund investors. These publications offer detailed analysis of funds, investing strategies, and how-to articles. Prices and publication frequency vary by publication. *Morningstar Funds 500* is an annual sourcebook ($35.00) that narrows the mutual fund universe from 15,000 to 500 funds ideal for building a diversified portfolio. *Morningstar FundInvestor* is a monthly, 48-page newsletter available in a print version ($99.00 for 12 issues) or electronic downloadable version ($89.00 for 12 issues). This newsletter is dedicated to helping investors pick the best mutual funds and build winning portfolios for greater gains.

MSN Money (*moneycentral.msn.com*)—This Web site offers news headlines, articles, quotes, and a wide range of online tools and resources for novice and serious investors alike. On this Web site, you'll find tools for managing a portfolio, planning for retirement, tracking investments, and conducting research about investments, including mutual funds. The services, articles, and tools are free of charge on this advertiser-supported site.

Mutual Fund Investor's Center (*www.mfea.com*)—Operated by the Mutual Fund Educational Alliance News Center, this Web site is a comprehensive resource for mutual fund investors. The "Investor Library" section features a series of how-to articles, covering topics like asset allocation, retirement planning, and taxes. The site also offers a free "Fund Selector" tool that can help you choose the best funds to invest in based on your needs, goals, and time horizon.

Securities and Exchange Commission (*www.sec.gov/investor/ pubs/inwsmf.htm*)—Obtain free information about mutual fund investing from the SEC. This Web page is a brochure entitled *Invest Wisely: An Introduction to Mutual Funds*.

The Motley Fool (*www.fool.com*)—Two brothers started offering investing advice in 1994 on American Online (AOL) to anyone who would listen. Known collectively as "The Motley Fool," they have written books, hosted radio shows on NPR, and shared their wisdom with countless investors. The Fool.com Web site offers an abundance of mutual fund-related advice, investing strategies, and tools. All of the content on this site is easy to understand, upbeat, and very informative. You can enter the mutual fund area of this site through *www.fool.com/school/mutualfunds/basics/intro.htm.*

The Wall Street Journal (800 568-7625 / *www.wsj.com*)— Offering both a daily printed newspaper and online edition, *The Wall Street Journal* is probably the most well-read and well-respected financial publication on the planet. Anyone who is interested in business, investing, or finance will find the articles and other information in this newspaper extremely valuable. The articles tend to be written in an easy-to-understand style. A one-year, print/online combination subscription is priced at $125. A one-year subscription to the printed newspaper is priced at $99.00 (including four free weeks). *The Wall Street Journal* is published Monday through Friday and is available from newsstands or by subscription. The Web site offers an abundance of information and tools for subscribers and non-subscribers alike.

Vanguard Group (*www.vanguard.com*)—The Web site of this full-service broker and mutual fund company offers an informative collection of how-to articles and online tools suitable for investors at all levels. Some of the tools are available only to shareholders or account holders.

Yahoo! Mutual Funds Center (*finance.yahoo.com/funds*)—You can access the latest news and information about mutual funds from this Web site, which is one component of Yahoo! Finance. This is an advertiser-supported site, so the content is available free of charge.

A P P E N D I X

Glossary

The following is a summary of popular mutual fund terms you'll want to be familiar with as you establish your portfolio and begin to manage your investments.

12b-1 Fees The percent of a mutual fund's assets assessed for marketing and distribution expenses, such as advertising, dealer compensation, and printing and mailing prospectuses and informational brochures.

The amount of the fee is stated in the fund's prospectus. These are also called *distributed fees.*

Account Maintenance Fees Fees charged by a mutual fund company to set up an account and/or maintain it. There may be a fee if the value of an account or the value of specific investments falls below a specific dollar level. Mutual fund companies will typically waive these account maintenance fees for investors with high-valued portfolios.

American College The organization that awards the professional designation of Chartered Financial Consultant (ChFC).

American Institute of Certified Public Accountants The organization that awards the professional designation of Certified Public Accountant (CPA).

Annual Percentage Rate (APR) A measure of the cost of credit, expressed as a yearly interest rate. All loans and forms of credit that charge interest have an APR.

Asset Allocation In a portfolio, the spread of investment money among types of assets.

Automatic Investment Plan Any arrangement that an investor sets up for a regular (monthly, quarterly, semiannual, or annual) withdrawal of money from a bank account to purchase shares in an investment, such as mutual funds.

Back-End Load A fee or commission charged to an investor who redeems shares in a mutual fund.

Bear Market A market in which the values of securities or commodities are persistently declining.

Beta A measure of a fund's or a stock's risk (volatility) relative to the market or another benchmark. The benchmark index has a beta of 1.0. A beta above 1.0 indicates that a fund's returns have fluctuated more than the benchmark index; a beta of below 1.0 indicates less fluctuation than the benchmark.

Blue-Chip Stock A generic term for the stocks of large companies (worth more than $3 billion) with a history of profitability, stability, and above-average performance. The name comes from poker, where the high-value chips are traditionally blue.

Broker An intermediary who is licensed to buy and sell securities through the stock exchanges.

Bull Market A market in which the values of securities or commodities are persistently rising.

Cap Market capitalization.

Capital Gain (Loss) An increase (decrease) in the value of a *capital asset* that puts that value above (below) the purchase cost. This gain (loss) is not realized (treated as real) until the capital asset is sold. A capital gain may be short term (one year or less) or long term (more than one year) and must be claimed as income. A mutual fund buys and sells investment assets. When a sale generates a profit and the asset was held by the fund for more than one year, that profit is capital gain, which is allocated among the fund's investors. Each investor receives a *capital gains distribution,* reported on a Form 1099-DIV. The distribution is taxed as a long-term capital gain regardless of how long the investor has owned the shares in the mutual fund.

Capital Gains Distribution The money paid by a mutual fund to each of its investors based on profits generated by the fund's investments. Capital gains distributions are typically distributed annually and reported on a Form 1099-DIV. The distribution is taxed as a long-term capital gain regardless of how long the investor has owned the shares in the mutual fund. Instead of receiving payment, an investor can opt to reinvest the capital gains distribution to acquire additional shares of the fund.

Capital Loss *See* **Capital Gain (Loss).**

Certified Financial Analyst (CFA) A financial planning expert who has been credentialed by the CFA Institute. It measures the competence and integrity of financial analysts. To obtain this accreditation, a person must have at least three years of work experience and pass three levels of exams covering areas such as accounting, economics, ethics, money management, and security analysis.

Certified Financial Planner (CFP) A financial planning expert who has been credentialed by the Certified Financial Planner Board of Standards. Not all financial planners are "certified." Only those people who have fulfilled the requirements of the CFP Board can use the CFP certification mark: they must complete the required education, pass a comprehensive certification exam, have a minimum of three years' experience as a financial planner, and adhere to the strict code of ethics mandated by the CFP Board. A CFP can serve as an investment or financial advisor, a money manager, or a portfolio manager, depending on his or her area of expertise.

Certified Financial Planner Board of Standards The organization that awards the professional designation of Certified Financial Planner (CFP).

CFA Institute The organization that awards the professional designation of Certified Financial Analyst (CFA).

Charitable Giving Type of investment allowing the investor to make tax-deductible donations with the dividends and capital gains distributions from mutual fund investments and/or donate the value of the investments themselves upon death. Many mutual fund companies can help you create a private foundation, make donations anonymously to your favorite charities, and/or donate your money however you choose.

Chartered Financial Consultant (ChFC) A financial planning expert who has been credentialed by The American College (*www.theamericancollege.edu*) after successfully completing courses in financial planning, investments, insurance planning, income taxation, retirement planning, and estate planning.

Churning The unethical practice of some investment advisors and brokers to increase their commissions by excessively trading in a client's account, a violation of the Fair Practice Rules of the National Association of Securities Dealers.

Closed-End(ed) Fund A mutual fund in which the fund manager has limited the number of shares. Unlike open-ended mutual funds, closed-end funds do not redeem their shares. The shares of a closed-end fund trade on the open securities market.

Constant Load An ongoing (annual) fee charged to an investor as long as he or she holds shares in a mutual fund. This can be in addition to a front-end load and/or back-end load as well as fees associated with the fund's expense ratio.

Credit Score A three-digit number between 300 and 850 that is calculated based on your credit (financial) reputation and history with creditors. Using a complex formula and many criteria related to your current financial situation and credit history, the three major credit reporting agencies calculate and regularly update your credit score.

Discretionary Income The money remaining after paying all monthly bills, expenses, and taxes.

Diversification The distribution of an investment portfolio across different investments as a strategy to reduce risk.

When a portfolio is diversified, if one investment declines in value, the chances are that the values of other investments will rise and offset that loss, since types of investments perform differently in various market or economic conditions. A well-diversified mutual fund portfolio would typically consist of stock funds, bond funds, and money market funds. It could be further diversified by investing in domestic, international, global, and/or sector- or industry-specific funds.

Dividend Payment by a stock-issuing company of a portion of earnings to its shareholders, determined by the board of directors. (Companies are not obligated to pay dividends.) Dividends can be paid in cash or in more stock. A dividend may be quoted in terms of the dollar amount for each share (*dividends per share*, DPS) or in terms of a percent of the current market price (*dividend yield*). When a mutual fund's holdings include stocks and those stocks pay dividends, the fund must pass those dividends along to the fund's investors annually. An investor must pay tax on this income. However, an investor has the option to automatically reinvest dividend payments, to acquire more shares.

DJIA *See* **Dow Jones Industrial Average**.

Dollar Cost Averaging An investment strategy consisting of investing an equal amount of money every month into a fund, regardless of the price of the fund. When the price is lower, the investment buys slightly more shares; when the price is higher, the investment buys slightly fewer shares.

This strategy results in lowering the average cost of a share if the price fluctuates up and down. It also decreases the risk of investing a large amount at the wrong time. When you sign up for an automatic investment plan, you'll be using this investment strategy.

Dow Jones Industrial Average (DJIA) A stock market index that consists of 30 of the largest and most widely held public companies in the United States and is used as a measure of how the stock market overall is performing. There are a variety of mutual funds designed to mimic the performance of this index.

Emerging Markets Fund A mutual fund that invests in companies in small, developing countries.

Exchange-Traded Fund A collective investment fund of securities that tracks an index, similar to an index fund, but is treated like an individual stock: shares are bought and sold through a broker and traded on an exchange during market hours.

Expense Ratio A measure of a mutual fund's total annual expenses expressed as a percentage of the fund's net assets. The lower the expense ratio, the better for the investor.

Federal Deposit Insurance Corporation An independent agency of the federal government created in 1933 to protect deposit accounts in case of bank failure, to maintain public confidence, and to promote stability in the financial system. The FDIC insures deposits of up to $100,000 in any member bank or thrift institution.

Front-End Load A fee or commission charged to an investor who buys shares in a mutual fund.

Fund Manager The person responsible for managing the money invested in a specific mutual fund and overseeing the day-to-day operation of that fund. The fund manager, with the help of analysts, decides how a fund's assets will be invested and what investment strategies will be used. When evaluating a mutual fund as a potential investment, consider the fund manager's experience, education, track record, investment strategy, and tenure managing that fund.

Fund of Funds A mutual fund that invests in other mutual funds. A fund of funds makes it easier for an investor to benefit from maximum diversification and achieve specific financial goals by investing into only one fund and reaping the benefits of several or many funds. Instead of paying fees for several funds, the fees tend to be a bit higher for a fund of funds because the investor is paying management fees twice.

Fund Selector (Screener) A type of online tool that searches through the 14,000-plus mutual funds to find those that meet whichever criteria the user has chosen, based on type, performance, risk, ratings, fund manager tenure, fees charged, or other factors. Free tools offer a few dozen search options, while some of the premium, fee-based tools offer 60 or more screening options, plus screens designed by experts to meet specific objectives.

Global Fund A mutual fund that invests in companies both in the United States and in other nations.

Hedge Fund A fund that is managed aggressively to get the highest returns by using derivatives and swaps, selling short, and working with other strategies. The funds typically attract investors with high net worth and institutions.

Holdings In mutual funds, the investments owned by a fund.

Index A hypothetical portfolio of securities intended to be representative of a particular market or sector of a market, to be used as a measure of changes in that market or sector and as a benchmark for measuring performance. The Dow Jones Industrial Average and the Standard & Poor's 500 are two of the best-known indexes and the benchmarks most commonly used for the U.S. stock market.

Index Fund A mutual fund intended to replicate the performance of the market or a sector by maintaining a portfolio of holdings that mirror the composition of a market or sector index. The most common index fund is based on the S&P 500, with holdings of all 500 stocks in the same percentages as the index. Other indexes that mutual funds emulate include the Russell 2000, the Wilshire 5000, and the NASDAQ 100. Index funds outperform most other mutual funds, in part because they are managed passively so their expenses are lower and in part because most managed mutual funds fail to perform better than broad indexes such as the S&P 500.

Investment Advisor Someone who helps an investor make investment decisions. This person can represent individual investors and charge a fee or can represent specific investment products, such as mutual funds, and generate sales commissions from selling investment products. Most mutual fund companies also employ salaried investment advisors who offer advice to clients.

Investment Advisor Representative A person employed by or associated with an investment advisor (company) who provides investment advice to clients. States use the Series 65 exam to test investment advisor representatives.

Joint Account An account opened by two people, who then share ownership of the account and its holdings in one of two ways.

Joint Tenants in Common Ownership by two or more people where a percentage of ownership is specified for each owner. If one owner dies, his or her share of the asset passes to his or her estate.

Joint Tenants with Rights of Survivorship Ownership by two or more people where there is no division of the asset. If one owner dies, total ownership passes to the surviving owner(s).

Large-Cap Stock Company with a market capitalization above $3 billion or $5 billion. These are well-established companies, like General Electric or IBM, which grow more slowly but are very stable.

Life-Cycle Fund A mutual fund in which the holdings change as time passes, using a systematic plan for adjusting asset allocation according to the target of the fund. Also known as *target-date fund* or *target-maturity fund*. For retirement investing, age-based life-cycle investing allows an investor to choose a fund based on a target date for retirement. As with any mutual fund, the mix of holdings will vary from fund to fund even if the funds have the same objective.

Liquidity The ease with which an investment can be converted into cash. Cash whether held in a traditional savings or checking account or stored under a mattress is the most liquid asset, because that money is readily available whenever you need it. A mutual fund investment is considered extremely liquid, because you can redeem your shares and receive cash quickly.

Load A fee or commission charged to an investor who buys or redeems shares in a mutual fund. The fee charged upon buying is called a *front-end* load and the fee charged on redeeming is called a *back-end* load.

Loaded Fund A mutual fund that charges fees.

Market Capitalization Total market value of a company, calculated as the number of shares outstanding multiplied by the current price of one share of the stock as quoted on a stock exchange. Capitalization is a common and convenient measure of the size of a company. In the U.S., there are generally three divisions of market capitalization, with varying dollar limits: large-cap (usually above $3 billion or $5 billion), mid-cap (usually between $500 million or $1 billion and $3 billion or $5 billion), and small-cap (usually below $500 million or $1 billion).

Maturity Length of time until the principal amount of a bond is to be repaid in full. This may be expressed in units of time or as a maturity date.

Mid-Cap Stock Company with a market capitalization between $500 million or $1 billion and $3 billion or $5 billion. These are typically more growth-oriented companies and are less risky than small-cap stocks but riskier than large-cap stocks.

Morningstar Style Box™ A graphic representation of a mutual fund in terms of three investment styles (small-cap stocks, mid-cap stocks, large-cap stocks) and three objectives (growth, value, blend both growth and value), forming a matrix of nine cells, one of which is highlighted. The Style Box characterizes a fund in one of nine ways: small-cap value, small-cap blend, small-cap growth, mid-cap value, mid-cap blend, mid-cap growth, large-cap value, large-cap blend, and large-cap growth.

NASDAQ National Association of Securities Dealers Automated Quotation System, designed for over-the-counter stock trading. Unlike the New York Stock Exchange and the American Stock Exchange, NASDAQ does not have a physical location for trading; trading is purely electronic, and all transactions happen over a network of computers and telephones.

National Association of Securities Dealers The primary private-sector regulator of America's securities industry. NASD licenses individuals and admits firms to the industry, writes rules to govern their behavior, examines them for regulatory compliance, and disciplines those who fail to comply. It oversees and regulates trading in equities, corporate bonds, securities futures, and options. It also provides education and qualification examinations to industry professionals.

Net Asset Value (NAV) The share price of a mutual fund. The NAV is calculated daily by adding up the values of all of the holdings in the fund portfolio and then subtracting any expenses associated with the management of the fund. This total value is then divided by the number of shares. Unlike a stock, a mutual fund can have an unlimited and ever-changing number of shares.

No-Load Fund A mutual fund that charges no fee or sales commissions for buying or selling shares.

Open-End(ed) Fund A mutual fund for which the number of shares available to investors is unlimited. It is possible for an open-end fund to stop accepting new investors.

Portfolio Either a collection of holdings of a mutual fund or a collection of investments held by an individual stocks, bonds, mutual funds, and other securities and assets (including cash).

Portfolio Asset Allocation The spread of investment money in a portfolio among types of assets.

Portfolio Management Tool An online or software application for tracking investments.

Prospectus A document that contains information about a specific mutual fund, including its costs, investment objectives, risks, details about the fund's manager, and information about the fund's past performance. You should read the prospectus thoroughly before investing.

R^2 A measure of how closely performance of a fund or a stock correlates with the performance of a benchmark index, expressed as a number between 0.00 and 1.00. An R^2 of 1.00 indicates a perfect correlation: all of the fluctuations of the fund or the stock match fluctuations of the index. An R^2 of 0.00 indicates that there's no correlation. If a fund had an R^2 of .47 relative to its benchmark, it would mean that 47 percent of its fluctuations match fluctuations in the benchmark. The lower the R^2, the greater the performance gap between the fund or the stock and the index; in other words, the more the fund or the stock reacts according to factors other than the factors that influence the market as measured by that benchmark.

Registered Investment Advisor (RIA) An investment advisor who is registered with the Securities and Exchange

Commission (SEC), which is generally a requirement when managing over $25 million in investments. Investment advisors who manage less than $25 million register with the securities regulatory agency in the state(s) in which they do business.

Return on Investment (ROI) A measure of the performance of an investment. The formula for calculating ROI is (gain from investment – cost of investment) ÷ cost of investment). The result is expressed as a percentage or a ratio. The higher the ROI, the better.

Risk In investing, the chance that the return on an investment will not be as expected. Risk for a specific investment is usually measured by calculating the standard deviation of the historical returns or the average returns of that investment. Generally, the riskier an investment, the greater the potential return on investment.

Risk Tolerance The degree of uncertainty that an investor can accept with regard to a decline in investment or portfolio value. Risk tolerance varies according to the investor's financial goals, time horizon, and so on.

S&P 500 A stock market index consisting of the stocks of 500 large corporations that trade on the major U.S. stock exchanges and are considered leaders in leading industries. The S&P 500 is an important index of large-cap U.S. stocks, second only to the Dow Jones Industrial Index. Many index funds track the performance of the S&P 500.

Security An investment product or vehicle that represents ownership, such as a mutual fund, stock, bond, option, or other type of financial asset.

Shareholder Report A document created by the mutual fund company for its shareholders that reveals fund performance and discloses information about the fund's holdings, investment strategies, expenses, and other details of interest to shareholders. This report can be issued annually, semiannually, or quarterly.

Small-Cap Stock Company with a market capitalization below $500 million or $1 billion. These are typically smaller, less established companies, which means investment is riskier.

Standard Deviation A measure of the variability of a fund's or a stock's returns over a period of time. The higher the standard deviation, the greater the variability. The calculation of standard deviation does not distinguish between gains and losses; it measures absolute variability, the degree of movement above or below the mean.

Style Box™, Morningstar See Morningstar Style Box™.

Time Horizon The length of time you'll be investing in order to reach a specific investment goal.

Total Return Percentage A measure of how much the value of an investment has increased or decreased during a specific time period.

Volatility In investing, the degree to which the value of an investment fluctuates, from hour to hour, day to day, week to week, month to month, or year to year. The value of an extremely volatile stock or mutual fund can go up and down quickly, often, and sometimes unexpectedly.

YTD Year to date.

Index

A

Account application
  personal contact information, 163-164
  process, 162-169
Annual percentage rate, 35
Automatic
  deductions, 166
  investment plan, 13, 17, 37

B

Bear market, 191
Beta, 136
Better Business Bureau, 64
Benz, Christine, interview, 143-152
Blue chip growth fund, 117-118
Blue chip stock, 84
Bond funds
  categories, 90

described, 89
diversified, 96
maturity, 90
BrokerCheck Hotline, 64
Bull market, 191

C

Cap, defined, 86
Capital gain, defined, 7
Capital gains distribution
  defined, 8
  taxes and, 11, 18
Certificate of deposit (CD), 91-92
Certified financial analyst (CFA), 57-58
Certified financial planner, 53, 58
Certified public accountant (CPA), 58
Charitable giving, 155

Charity, and mutual funds, 22
Charles Schwab, 52, 53, 65-66
Chartered financial consultant
  (CHFC), 58
Checking, deductions from, 167
Churning, 64
Closed-end funds, 6, 114
CNN Money Mutual Fund
  Screener, 133
College, saving for, 23
Country-specific mutual funds,
  87
Credit score, 34

D
Debt, paying off, 28
Discretionary income, 29
Diversification
  composition of portfolio, 142
  defined, 4
  going overboard, 146
  as mutual fund advantage, 9
  reducing risk, 48
  Ritter, comments on, 71-73
Dividends
  and capital gains distribu-
    tions, 107
  defined, 7
  taxes and, 11
Dollar cost averaging, 17, 152
Domini Social Investments, 95
Dow Jones Industrial Average
  (DJIA), 87, 88
Dreyfus S&P 500 Index, 92

E
Emerging markets funds, 97
Equity growth funds, 97
Estate planning, 23
Exchange-treaded funds
  goal, 114-115
  history of , 114
  information sources, 115-116
Expense ratio, 16, 18

F
Federal Trade Commission, 34
Fees
  12B-1, 114
  analyzing, 112-114
  commissions, 106
  and expenses of fund, 105
  listed, 105-106
  look for low, 49
  maintenance, 18, 157
  social, 95
  understanding, 65-67
Fidelity Compare Funds tool,
  135
Fidelity Investments, 16, 52, 53,
  65-66, 92, 157-158
Financial goals
  investing enough to achieve,
    39
  long- and short-term, 37-39,
    44-46
  worksheets, 38, 45-46
Financial situation, personal
  analyzing, 29-36

Flora, John, interview, 186-189
Forbes Fund Screener, 133
Fund evaluation, considerations, 147-148
Fund manager, 11, 108, 148
Fund of funds, 79, 96
Fund selection, narrowing, 131-134

G
goodfunds.com, 95
Growth funds, 97

H
Hedge fund, 144
High-yield bond funds, 97
Historical performance, 6

I
Index funds, 88, 92-93
Initial investment minimum, 50
International bond funds, 97
International funds, portfolio allocation, 199
International growth funds, 97
Investing, mutual funds, ten basic steps, 175-176
Investment advisor
  certification, 57-60
  checking credentials, 62-64
  defined, 14
  finding through referral, 57
  questions to ask, 60-62
  investment plan and, 56
  need for, 54-55

primary responsibilities, 194-195
public disclosure Web site, 63
selecting, 56-57
Investment Company Institute, 2
Investment goals
  defining for self, 28
  reviewing, 159
  and strategy, 146-147
Investment objective of fund, 104
Investment strategy of fund, 104

J
Joint accounts
  applying, 163
  defined, 164
  types, 164

L
Large-cap stock, 87
Large-company value funds, 97
Life-cycle fund, 73, 85
Liquidity
  defined, 11
  as mutual fund advantage, 10
LiveStrong Portfolios, 94

M
Management software tools
  ES Quotes, 183
  free, 179
  FundBuilder, 184
  Fund Manager software package, 17, 183

Management software tools
(*continued*)
and inputting data, 182
Microsoft Money Deluxe, 184
MSN Money Investment
Toolbox, 184-185
mutual fund company offer-
ings, 180
offered by Morningstar, 180-
182
offered by Vanguard, 195
Palm OS Smartphone, 186
Quicken Premiere, 185
SmartMoney.com, 185-186
Market capitalization, 86
McLaughlin, Michael, interview,
193-199
Mid-cap stock, 87
Minimum investment, 36, 107
Mistakes made by investors,
196-197
Money held by broker, 170
Money market funds, 91-92
Morningstar
Benefits, 182
Instant X-Ray, 141
mutual fund analyst, 84
offerings for investors, 143-
144
portfolio management tool,
180-182
star ratings, 145
Style Box^{TM}, 140, 149-150
tools offered by, 137-140

using, 121
Web site, 144
Motley Fool, 93
Mutual fund company
choosing, 156-158
contact information, 159
directory, 160
portfolio management tools
offered, 180
resources for investors, 74-75
Mutual funds
advantages, investing, 9-10
attractiveness to investors, 70,
119-120, 145-146
bond, 89-91
classified by strategy, 84-85
company, choosing, 156-159
country-specific, 87
defined, 3-4
drawbacks, 10-12, 70-71
ease of investing, 12
establishing account, 162-163
evaluating, 77-78, 120-121
experience of investing, 26
fees, 18
index, 88, 92-93
investing, ten basic steps, 175-
176
liquidity, 10
management, 10
misconceptions, 150-151
money market, 91-92
objectives, 8-9, 83
prospectus, 14-15, 16

regulation, 10
researching, 124-153
research tools, 78
screener tools, 133-134
sector, 93-94
security of, 9
shareholder information, 106
six questions to ask before
    investing, 111-112
why people invest, 21-24

N

National Association of
    Securities Dealers, 63
Net asset value, 5, 18-19
No-load funds
    defined, 20
    fees, 18

O

One-stop shops, 52, 193
Open-end funds, 6, 114

P

Palm OS Smartphone, 186
Passive investing, 55
Past performance of fund
    prospectus information, 105
    selection based on, 129
Personal goals, 41-42
Portfolio
    defined, 4
    keeping stable, 192
    management. *See* Portfolio
    management

management software tool,
    172, 177, 178-179
periodic review, 76-77, 122
purposeful, 170
Portfolio asset allocation
    aggressive growth, 101-102
    balanced, 100-101
    conservative, 100
    defined, 83
    extremely aggressive growth,
    102
    growth, 101
    importance of , 98-99
    short-term, 99
Portfolio management
    benchmarks, 191
    gathering information, 177-
    178
    periodic checks, 176-177, 190
    reasons for, 174
    tips, 197-198
    tool for, 137
Principles for Responsible
    Investing, 95
Professional goals, 45-46
Prospectus
    anatomy of, 103-108
    defined, 16
    obtaining, 14-15
    reading, 19, 102-103
Puglia, Larry J., interview, 84,
    116-122

Q

Quicken
  Flora, John, senior product
    manager, 186-187
  portfolio management tool,
    185
Quotes, sources of, 140-140

R

R^2, 136
Rate of return, 6, 47
Reasons people invest in mutu-
  al funds, 21-24
Registered investment advisor
  (RIA), 58-59
Reinvesting, dividends and cap-
  ital gains, 166
Researching mutual funds
  Fund Evaluator^{SM}, 132
  fund selection,
  fund selector tool, 126-127
  importance of, 127-128
  know sources of information,
    131
  Morningstar tools for, 130,
    132-133
  portfolio tips, 126
  six things to know about
    fund, 130
Research tools
  asset allocator, 136
  CNN Money Mutual Fund
    Screener, 133

cost analyzer, 137
Fidelity Compare Funds, 135
Forbes Fund Screener, 133
fund screener, 134
portfolio allocator, 137
portfolio manager, 137
risk analyzer, 137
SmartMoney Fund Finder,
  134
use of, 78
Yahoo! Finance Mutual Fund
  Screener, 134
Retirement, 23
Return on investment (ROI), 19
Risk, 3, 18, 24, 46-50, 79-80
Risks of fund, 104
Ritter, Stuart, interview, 54, 67-
  80

S

Safety and time horizon, 142
Sector funds, 93-94
Securities and Exchange
  Commission
  checking on advisors, 62-63
  website, 5
Shareholder report
  defined, 20
  components of, 109-111
Small-cap stock, 86
Small-company funds, 97
Smart Debt (Jason Rich), 33
SmartMoney Fund Finder, 134
Social fees, 95

SocialFunds.com, 95
Spartan 500 Index Fund, 16, 92
Specialty funds, 94-96
Standard deviation (fund volatility), 136
Standard & Poor's 500 Index, 16, 87, 88
Stock funds, 85-89

T
Tax bracket, 36
Tax consequences of fund, 107-108
Time horizon, 13, 40
T. Rowe Price, 52, 53, 65-66, 67, 68, 74, 92, 99

V
Vanguard, 53, 65-66, 92

Volatility
beta, 136
defined, 47
standard deviation, 136

W
Wealth, building, 21, 24-25
Worksheets
current debt, 32
investment goals, 161-162
monthly income, 30
portfolio, 171
total monthly expenses, 31
total savings, 30

Y
Yahoo! Finance
free prospectus service, 109
mutual fund screener, 134

Other Books by Jason R. Rich from Entrepreneur Press

The following books are now available wherever books are sold or can be ordered through the EntrepreneurPress.com Web site. For more information about these and other books written by bestselling author Jason R. Rich, visit his Web site at www.JasonRich.com.

202 High-Paying Jobs You Can Land Without a College Degree .
Smart Debt

Entrepreneur Magazine's Pocket Guides
Dirty Little Secrets: What the Credit Bureaus Won't Tell You
Why Rent? Own Your Dream Home
Mortgages and Refinancing: Get the Best Rates
Buy or Lease a Car Without Being Taken for a Ride (2007)
Get that Raise! (2007)

Entrepreneur Magazine's Business Traveler Series
Entrepreneur Magazine's Business Traveler Guide to Las Vegas
and coming soon ...
Entrepreneur Magazine's Business Traveler Guide to Washington, DC
Entrepreneur Magazine's Business Traveler Guide to New York City
Entrepreneur Magazine's Business Traveler Guide to Orlando
Entrepreneur Magazine's Business Traveler Guide to Chicago
Entrepreneur Magazine's Business Traveler Guide to Los Angeles